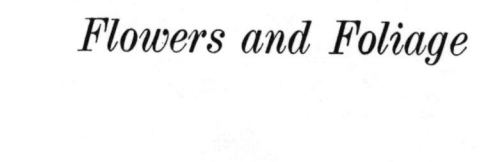

Flowers and Foliage

Flowers and Foliage
Creative Compositions

Nora Fields

SOUTH BRUNSWICK AND NEW YORK: A. S. BARNES AND COMPANY
LONDON: THOMAS YOSELOFF LTD

© 1973 by A. S. Barnes and Co., Inc.

A. S. Barnes and Co., Inc.
Cranbury, New Jersey 08512

Thomas Yoseloff Ltd
108 New Bond Street
London W1Y OQX, England

Library of Congress Cataloging in Publication Data

Fields, Nora.
  Flowers and foliage.

  1. Flower arrangement. I. Title.
SB449.F48   745.92'24   71-39828
ISBN 0-498-01162-3

Printed in the United States of America

*To my husband,
Samuel Bernard Fields,
and my daughters Melinda and Nanette.
Their cooperation and patience made
this book possible.*

Contents

Foreword 9
Preface 11

Section I
How to Enjoy the Flower Arrangements of Today 15

Section II
How to Create the Flower Arrangements of Today 39

1 Design 41
2 Plant Material to Grow 57
3 Forcing Shrubs and Trees 78
4 Conditioning of Fresh Plant Material 83
5 Preserving and Treating Plant Material 93
6 Driftwood and Weathered Wood 107
7 Containers 120
8 Basic Mechanics 139
9 Occasions for Flower Arranging 144
   Index 159

Foreword

There is something of the poet's verbal sensitivity that is expressed in the visual enchantment of the flower arranger's art. William Blake delightfully describes the pleasures of a flower garden in his poem "Song":

> He show'd me lilies for my hair
> And blushing roses for my brow;
> He led me through his garden fair
> Where all his golden pleasures grow.

Nora Fields in this volume brings us the awareness of this beauty and joy in flowers through her arrangements in formal patterns of delicate and sensitive relationships in color, form and line.

All of us take pleasure in the sight of the wild flowers of the field and those cultivated in our gardens, but often we find ourselves inadequate in arranging aesthetic displays in our homes and for the occasions where flowers are an important element of an environment.

In this informative book, Nora Fields, whose teaching has for years benefited and inspired countless students, helps the reader to better enjoy and evaluate flower displays everywhere and, most importantly, to develop the understanding and skills which will enable one to design, create, and preserve eloquent and pleasurable flower displays for the delight of all.

John Ruddley
Westchester County Supervisor of Art;
Director of the Westchester Art Workshop,
Department of Parks, Recreation, and
Conservation, Westchester County, New York

Preface

Although related elements are involved in enjoying, creating, showing, and judging the flower arrangements of today, these terms are not synonymous, nor is TODAY like YESTERDAY or TOMORROW. As in any of the arts, you can, for a wide variety of reasons, engage in many phases of an activity quite successfully without indulging in the others.

Perhaps the key word here is "enjoy," because whether you are a participant in creating or judging flower arrangements, or whether you are a spectator looking at them, God's bounty should provide a source of enjoyment and enrichment. And if you react with pleasure to the beauty of flowers, enjoyment can be increased by a familiarity with the concept of flower arranging as an art.

This book was written to sharpen your perception, imagination, and knowledge, to broaden your perspective with a wide-angle lens instead of a narrow one, and to stimulate you to try your skills in new ventures. It is within each of us to create, share, and see new vistas of beauty—or chaos.

Flowers and Foliage

SECTION I
*How to Enjoy
the Flower Arrangements
of Today*

Whether you enjoy flower arrangements at home or at a flower show, the variety and depth of your background and the openness of your spirit will greatly influence what you see.

Everyone who enjoys listening to music, every critic who evaluates music, is not necessarily a performing musician, or, even if he is, is not equally adept at piano, voice, wind and string instruments. And every musician is not necessarily a perceptive critic.

It is true that as a performer or as an artist you have a greater understanding of what goes into an outstanding composition. But enjoying, judging, and evaluating call for additional insights—and, in fact, one's own approach or technique may color what one expects of others.

"I know what I like" is often the criterion, sometimes a valid one, for one should not be influenced to the point of having formed no personal opinion; but this is generally not the best criterion for evaluating the works of others. It is also important to remember that everything created is not necessarily good, just as "if it appears in print it must be true" is, of course, obviously factitious.

To look at an Ikenobo Rikka (plate 1), for example, one might see rhythm and beauty; but some knowledge of the nine line-placements basic to this particular specialized design will greatly enhance one's enjoyment. To know that this is one of the most difficult and most complex of the formal Japanese designs adds greatly to one's understanding and appreciation, as does the knowledge that a singer with a two-octave range is excellent but one with a three-octave range is unusual.

This classical Ikenobo Rikka by Mary Takahashi is a dramatic six-foot composition. In its nine placements, it features the bare deciduous branches of early spring, evergreens, white iris, and white daisies.

In discussing the enjoyment of modern flower arranging, we must first determine just what "enjoyment" entails. According to Webster it means: "1. having or experiencing with joy; getting pleasure from; 2. having the use of or benefit of something; having as one's lot or advantage."

Thus the often heard comment, "I wouldn't have that thing in my house," while highly subjective and not entirely rational as an evaluation, does have some basis, whether it applies to a flower arrangement, a painting, a sculpture, or a piece of furniture.

Enjoyment, however, although highly subjective, still requires the broader basis of understanding. If you look at hieroglyphics, you may "enjoy" the visual pattern, but much greater enjoyment would come from being able to "read" the message. This subtle difference can be clearly appreciated within the framework of the Concrete Poetry Movement, as seen in plate 2 from *Street Poems* by Robert Froman.

If you listen to music, melody may give you great enjoyment; but knowing the score, reading the libretto, listening to the counterpoint, the range, the tonal values, knowing something about the composer and the performing artists, will all enhance your enjoyment.

If you read a flower show schedule and know that the exhibitor is in a class called "Greenwich Village" (plate 3), that she was permitted to use a combination of fresh and dried plant material, and that the rules of that particular class also permitted the use of an accessory, this can greatly enhance and enrich your perception and enjoyment when you look at the arrangement.

1 IKENOBO RIKKA by Mary Takahashi (Photo by Alwood Harvey)

THE CITY QUESTION

Man on face on sidewalk. Wino? Junkie? Hurt? Sick? Knife in pocket? Danger? Medicine in pocket? May die without it?

Forget him?

Leave him to the cops?

Or try to help?

2 "The City Question" from *Street Poems* by Robert Froman. Reprint by permission of McCall Books.

3 GREENWICH VILLAGE (Photo by C. Everett Garvey)

How to Enjoy the Flower Arrangements

In trying to express the essence of Greenwich Village, New York, with plant material in this blue ribbon arrangement, pampas grass was bent to suggest the skyscrapers which surround the Village, mullein seed pods were used to reinforce the lines and give weight and stability to the composition, three weathered bricks formed a base to express the brick stoops, with a square cup-pinholder which was painted to look like another brick. The red geraniums and their bright green foliage suggested the window boxes often found in that part of New York City. And the beautifully carved wooden sculpture by Anri of a little girl playing "he loves me, he loves me not" with a daisy suggested the universal quality of youth and hope.

It is also important to remember that creative ability or knowledge in one area does not imply equal understanding or ability in other areas. Frequently the study of a new medium will give rise to a new artistic outlet for a creative person; but in transposing from one art to another, the true essential qualities of each medium must be thoroughly understood, considered, and mastered.

Judges and performing artists, as well as sophisticated gallery critics, often become overly critical and demanding. One of the best art teachers with whom I studied in college gave up his own creative painting because his critical evaluations were developed too far beyond his ability to produce and create. He thus developed a lack of appreciation for the very basis or "grass-roots" of creativity, for skill will only develop through practice. It may be important to have your eye on the stars, but one must still retain a rapport with humanity.

Conversely, every creative effort, even by the great masters, could not possibly be a masterpiece. All creative art is based upon reaction: to the past, to the materials used, to one's training and ability, and to the efforts put forth separately in each individual endeavor.

Modern artists were once criticized as being unable to draw, hence they had to create distortions; but a study of Pablo Picasso, for example, will clearly show that his technique developed from realistic and academic training and traditions to the simplifications and, later, from the distortions based upon further design simplifications and patterns—his personal reaction to our fragmented world. Examine plates 4 and 5.

"The Gourmet," painted in 1901, was a realistic masterpiece from his "blue period." Contrast this with his cubistic "The Mirror," painted in 1932. And these are but two of the many styles which have evolved from the brush of this prolific artist.

A study of other contemporary artists will show that they, too, have undergone similar evolutionary processes in developing their own techniques and distinctive styles.

You do not have to want a particular composition to enjoy it. If it gives you food for thought, if it is provocative, if it was an aesthetic experience to look at, you have enjoyed it.

The composition in plate 6, using "fresh field and roadside material," was itself hampered by several residual and implied considerations. No plant material on the local state conservation list may be used in any National Council standard flower show, although much of this abounds in field and roadside. In addition, this type of native plant material is quite difficult to condition and is frequently not hardy enough to hold up for a long period of time, an important prerequisite for anything used in a summer show.

Queen Anne's lace was used in its green unopened state, with dock for line, green sumac berries, and velvety green mullein foliage with a piece of weathered wood which had interesting holes in it and was mounted on a rusty pipe set in a natural burl base. The entire composition was in shades of green and brown. This blue ribbon arrangement is one which you may or may not want to have in your home, but you could enjoy it in a particular setting.

During the Middle Ages, many great tapestries were created to warm (physically as well as aesthetically) medieval castle halls. One series of outstanding examples can be found at the Cloisters in New York City (the famous Unicorn tapestries). You must go there to enjoy them.

Many great sculptures were created for herculean settings; *e.g.*, Michelangelo's "Moses" for the tomb of Pope Julius II.

Many great sculptures look cramped and crowded even in their museum settings; some were created as outdoor garden pieces, with the sky, not a roof, for their ceiling. Some, like Calder's mobiles, were meant to move in the passing breeze.

4 THE GOURMET by Pablo Picasso

Impossible Art of today, the decorating of an outdoor facade of a building with canvas and cloth or a field that is excavated and contoured, is not new. Its feet rest in the examples of nature's magnificence as seen in Bryce Canyon in Utah, or in the man-made sculptures at Mount Rushmore, South Dakota, or in the contour-plowed and landscaped fields of a Japanese hillside. Although Earthworks is not necessarily an approach to art which has any degree of lasting permanence, it does recur from time to time in the personal expression and reaction of various artists.

Through the years, as consumers of art scaled their living from castles and cathedrals to great halls and mansions and then to split levels, apartments, and condominiums, the scale and proportion of the artists' creations have changed also. In the development of the art of flower arranging in Japan, for example, the great temple and court Rikkas made exclusively by men were scaled down to the more modest Shoka patterns as well as Moribana designs and modern Rikkas created by artists of both sexes which fit into the average home location much more readily. Thus perhaps as far back as at its primeval source, all art needed to be wanted, used and housed.

The modern Ikenobo Rikka shown in plate 7 has many of the same basic lines and placements as the classical Rikka, but it is scaled down in technique and proportion to a much less formal design. This Gendai Rikka features pussy willow, eucalyptus, pink heather, pink azalea, and pink iris.

5 THE MIRROR by Pablo Picasso

Op Art is often considered new, but optical illusion is one of nature's oldest tricks. Observe the natural camouflage of the zebra, the moth. Application of this universal principle is used

6 **FIELD AND ROADSIDE FLOWERS** (Photo by Daniel Berry)

7 GENDAI RIKKA (Photo by George E. Ernst)

8 **WEED RIKKA (Photo by James Swan)**

9 PARTY FOR SWINGERS by Melinda Sue Fields
(Photo by George E. Ernst)

How to Enjoy the Flower Arrangements

today for totally different reasons. Remember the trees of Birnam Woods in *Macbeth?* Remember the camouflaged installations used by soldiers in Korea, Vietnam, Cambodia? As our knowledge of nature's principles develops, these principles can be applied in illusions.

The principle of after-image and illusion was utilized by the Impressionists who used the viewer's eye to fuse and blend unrelated color. Interesting effects can be achieved and understood when this technique is applied. Try staring at a dot of red long enough and your eye will fatigue, causing you to see red's opposite, or green.

Those who use the criterion, "I cannot enjoy it because it is not beautiful," should perhaps be reminded that beauty is often seen in the eye of the beholder.

Are weeds beautiful? Perhaps they can be, or at least can be used to create, an interesting design, as in plate 8, which features grasses, clover, Queen Anne's lace and wild violet foliage.

What we find beautiful may be determined by past experience and exposure. To the Japanese traditionalist, the term "shibui," which means muted colors and subtle harmonies, implies beauty, as seen in the subtle coloration of the female cardinal, not the flamboyant male. To modern youth of today, in any country, hot psychedelic colors and harmonies are exciting and beautiful.

The Ashcan school of art developed back in the time of John Sloan when mundane and unattractive things were imbued with a new beauty because of the sensitivity and artistically perceptive eye of the artist.

Perhaps we are in a new and similar stage in flower arranging today with *objets trouvés* playing an important part in compositions, both as unusual containers and unusual accessories. Perhaps this also is the final answer to today's vast problem of what to do with our great industrial and personal discards. "It ain't what you do, it's the way that you do it." A cliché, yes, but one which makes us aware of how important the artist or designer is in creating any composition.

"Partly for Swingers" (plate 9) was created by Melinda Sue Fields, who was fifteen years old at the time. The container was an old, scratched l.p. record (plate 10). It took about twenty min-

utes for the record to melt over a glass jar in the oven, which had been set at 300°. A cup-pin-holder, painted black, held the red gladioli and the dried branch, to which a pre-formed black "flower" 45rpm record was attached. This arrangement was exhibited at the International Flower Show in New York in a section devoted exclusively to the work of qualified juniors and high school gardeners. It was not in competition.

10 **RECORD** (Photo by Alwood Harvey)

In flower forms, beauty, which adds so much to enjoyment, can be in the intrinsic pattern of lines and color, as seen in a rubrum lily; it can be in the dignity of a calla lilly, the ruffled form of a petunia, or the brightness and freshness of a daisy. It can be in the bold simplicity of a piece of fruit or in nature's sculptures of driftwood.

The driftwood fish in plate 11 was whittled a little to enhance its natural form and a few small pieces of wood were glued to the basic form. Then the entire piece was mounted on a piece of metal. The "seaweed" into which it seems to swim was made of scrap metal shavings and the wire springs of a spiral notebook, with glass floats and martynia pods.

There is beauty in the depth and texture of a velvet rose, but beauty should not be confused with prettiness. There is beauty in dry pods, twisted branches, a rock, a shell, a piece of coral. But a full measure of beauty without the relief of

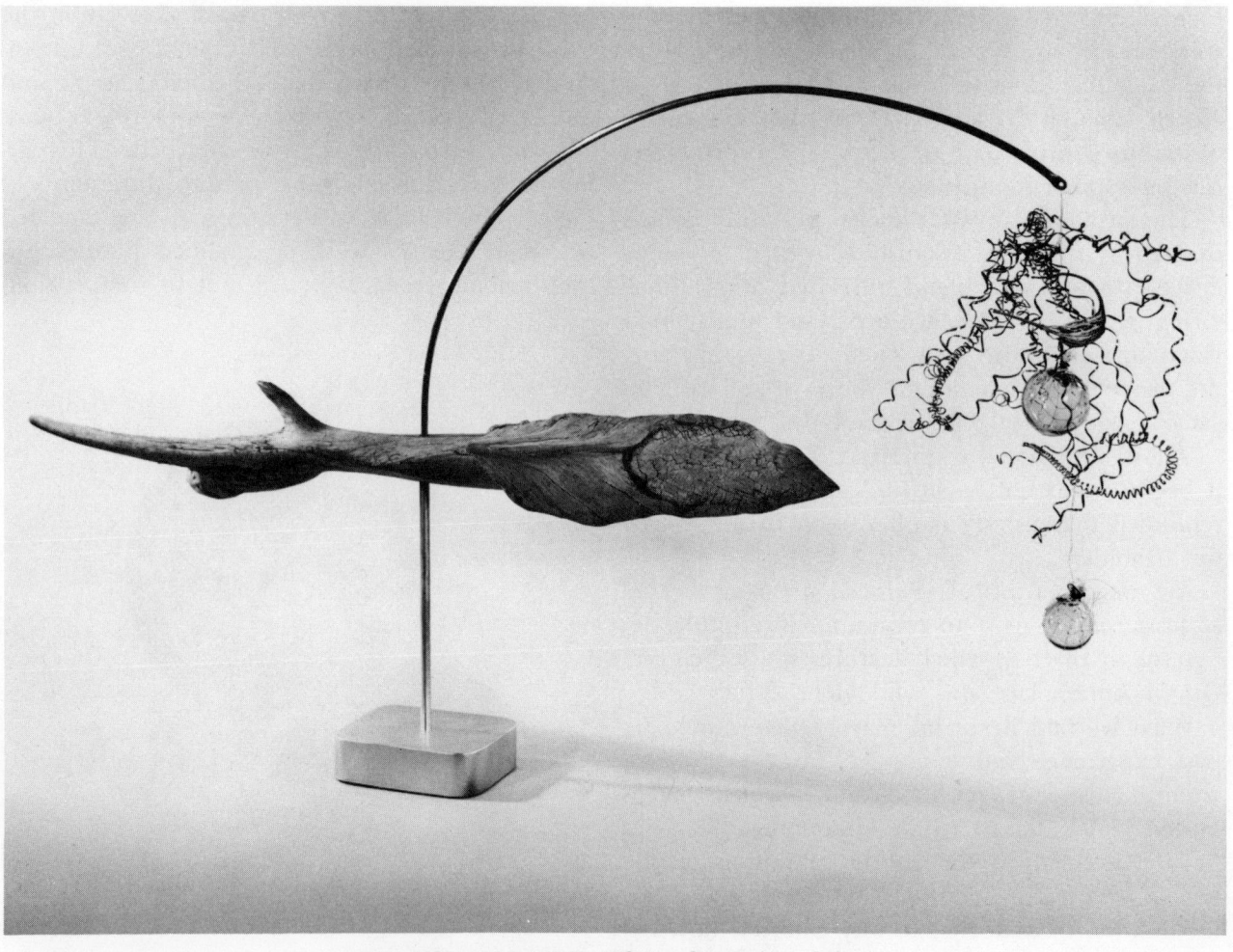

11 FISH MOBILE (Photo by James Swan)

other material and without the control of good design would be like a meal consisting entirely of dessert. It is only through contrast of opposites, balance and counterpoint, and the controlling forces of a good composition that we can place beauty in its proper setting and fully enjoy it in its many forms.

Two beautiful abalone shells (plate 12) were mounted on a metal pipe to which an interesting curl of scrap steel from a knife factory was added. Mounting the shells emphasizes their beauty and importance. Using them as a container for the flowers would minimize them, therefore a cup-pinholder was used to hold pink gladioli and gladiolus foliage. Two curls of wisteria bent over a bottle to repeat the curl of the steel *objet trouvé* complete the composition.

The aesthetics of all your experiences and knowledge enter into your basic concepts to color your enjoyment. If you look at a printed page and cannot read, you cannot obtain enjoyment from the verse, the style, or the ideas presented. The totally uninitiated, the totally untrained can only get the simplest and most obvious enjoyment from a symphony. The more you grow and develop through personal trial and error and through experience, the greater will be your sensitivity, your "vibrations," and the more diversified will be your enjoyment from any experience, whether it be watching a ballet or a baseball game or attending a flower show.

Since knowledge and understanding are of importance to enjoyment, there are a few questions or criteria you can use to evaluate the quality

12 **ABALONE SHELLS** (Photo by George E. Ernst)

13 **MINIATURE** by Melinda Sue Fields (Photo by Alwood Harvey)

of a given creative endeavor, so that in turn you may discover to what degree it is "enjoyable":

1. Is it right in its *raison d'etre*, its interpretation, its theme, its very existence?

2. Is it right in its use, placement and application, its scale and proportion, its frame of reference? (Would you enjoy a miniature alone on a grand piano or a five-foot assemblage on your small tea table?)

An example of this is the small blue ribbon arrangement in plate 13, which measured well under five inches in height, by Melinda Sue Fields, who was thirteen at the time. It utilizes heather, pruned to look like a tree and set in a tiny pinholder clayed into a bottle cap, and a small horn carving of a bird. The base was a thin sliver of slate. Scale and proportion are of great importance, and a good design should be so well coordinated that all the component parts in the composition are in perfect relationship to each other.

3. Does it fit the scene today? At one time magazine photographs and illustrations had a margin around them; today the more subjective and intimate technique of cropping or bleeding a picture to the edge of the page is used, even bringing the viewer closer by cutting off part of the subject to create more emphasis.

4. Does it express and reflect its period in history or evolution? Venus de Milo was considered the ideal woman when she was created; today she would go on a crash diet. What one period considers ideal, beautiful, perfect, or enjoyable is not necessarily ideal for another. The generation gap is not new; we have always reacted to the past, rebelled against it, and thus carved the path within which we have created new forms, new concepts, new mores, new arts. We progress in elliptical patterns.

Nudes in sculpture in our permissive culture are scarcely given a second glance; topless waitresses rate little more attention. But in the Victorian period even chaste "September Morn" was considered risqué. And plastered fig leaves were applied to strategic parts of the anatomy of Greek and Roman sculptures in museums throughout the world.

5. Is it honest in its application of materials and sound in its construction? Will it hold up or wear well? A Christmas door decoration of crepe paper could not possibly weather the elements and therefore would not be a structurally sound creation.

6. Is the craftsmanship, the basic mechanics of construction, suitable to the above concepts? Technique is not always the same. In painting,

14 **SELF PORTRAIT by Albrecht Dürer (From the Prado Museum)**

some artists (Vincent Van Gogh) used a pallet knife, some (Georges Seurat) used the tip of a brush to create little dots of color which the eye blends visually, some (Willem de Kooning) used a spatter technique and even threw paint upon the canvas, some (Salvador Dali) used long brush strokes to smoothly blend the paint. Each artist used different techniques in achieving self-expression. No one approach is "right" or "wrong" as

15 **WHEATFIELDS** by Jacob van Ruisdael (From The Metropolitan Museum of Art. Bequest of Benjamin Altman, 1913)

such. All can be enjoyed under the right circumstances.

7. Is the design sound? Design principles of scale and proportion, rhythm and balance, and dominance and contrast remain the same; they are timeless concepts. But their application and emphasis in the use of the design elements (line, form, texture, pattern, color, and space relationships) changes constantly throughout the ages as well as within the framework of each individual's application.

For a frame of reference, it is interesting to remember that in Albrecht Dürer and Leonardo Da Vinci's time, landscape painting was considered suitable only as a background; although they painted with such care and attention to details that we can actually recognize botanical specimens and even rock formations, it remained a background in the composition (plate 14). It was not until the time of the little Dutch masters, such as Jacob van Ruisdael and Pieter Bruegel, that landscapes became suitable subject matter for a whole composition (plate 15).

Contrast the "Self Portrait" by Albrecht Dürer (plate 14) with the "Wheatfields" by Jacob van Ruisdael. (plate 15). In the first, the focus is

MAGNOLIA MOBILE (Photo by James Swan)

HOLOCAUST (Photo by George E. Ernst)

ECOLOGY (Photo by George E. Ernst)

PEONIES AND WOOD (Photo by George E. Ernst)

How to Enjoy the Flower Arrangements 33

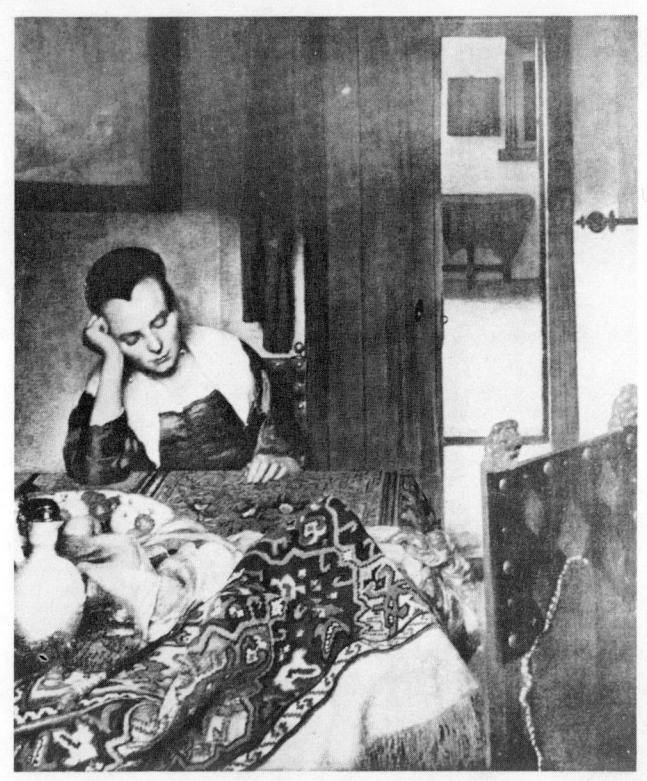

16 GIRL ASLEEP by Johannes Vermeer (From The Metropolitan Museum of Art. Bequest of Benjamin Altman, 1913)

17 GIRL HOLDING A FLOWER BASKET by Jean Germain Drouais

18 TULIPS IN A VASE by Paul Cézanne

19 **APPLES** (Photo by Alwood Harvey)

How to Enjoy the Flower Arrangements

entirely on the portrait; in the other, although several people are painted on the road, the focus is entirely upon the landscape.

Still life, too, was considered just a part of the overall composition, indicative of a homey atmosphere, even into the time of Johannes Vermeer. But Pieter de Hooch, Jean Baptiste Chardin, and still later Paul Cézanne elevated genre to the level of subject matter worthy of a painting.

Contrast the arrangement of fruit in "Girl Asleep" (plate 16) by Johannes Vermeer, the importance and use of flowers in the portrait of "A Girl Holding a Flower Basket" by Jean Germain Drouais in plate 17, and the painting of "Tulips in a Vase" by Paul Cézanne (plate 18), where the fruit, foliage, and flowers comprise the subject matter entirely on their own in a dynamic composition.

It is interesting to note that the Empress Josephine, Napoleon's wife, created flower arrangements during her studies with the artist Pierre Redouté so that she could produce a composition which was worth painting.

8. Is there an essence of creativity in it or is this just a rehash of someone else's ideas, old or new?

In the modern design a la Mondrian in plate 19, created for a lecture demonstration, the artist's approach (plate 20) was used for inspiration, but the arrangement was transposed into the three-dimensional medium of the flower arranger. The framework is the "container," which was constructed to hold the red Delicious apples in place. Yellow daffodils in two cup-pinholders were also utilized. Thus, the strong spatial relationships, the use of primary color, the abstract geometric forms, the very essence of Piet Mondrian was distilled but not copied, for no two media and no two artists are any more alike than any two fingerprints.

The great danger here, however, is that anyone can become insatiable, too sophisticated, too demanding. Few things are "new" and few of today's artistic endeavors will be ranked as great 100 years from now. Few artists have truly contributed to new concepts and new trends; there are few Alexander Calders or Henry Moores.

In the table mobile in plate 21, created for a flower show school demonstration, the essence of mobility a la Calder was used to establish a composition in the medium of the flower arranger. This could not be merely flat black metal pieces, but must include both color and three-dimensional natural objects.

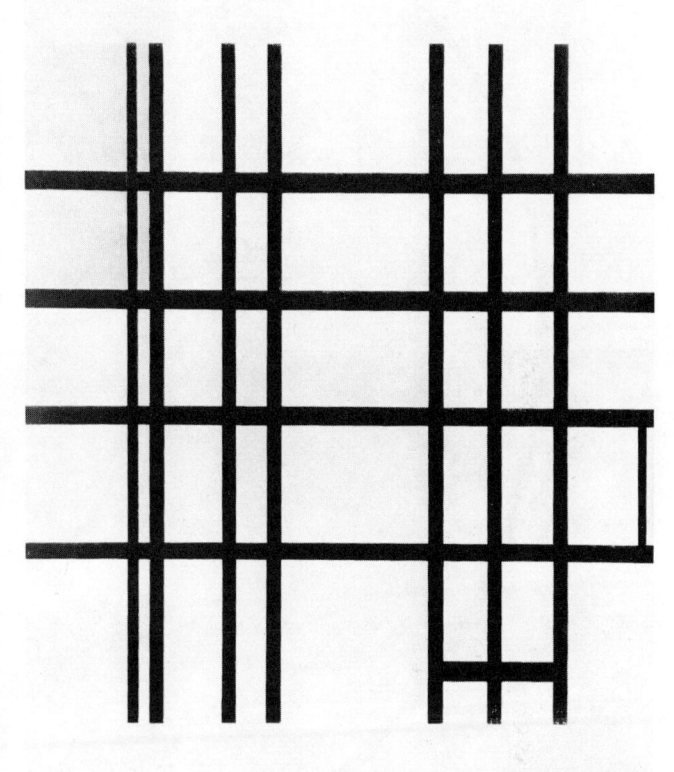

20 SPACE AND PATTERN by Piet Mondrian

Two bent forsythia branches, some foliage, an aqua pick and a copper tube to hold the flowers in water, two small birds, thread, coat hanger wire, and weights, all were combined to create a design in which every part moves in the slightest air current. A slight physical imbalance is necessary to keep this type of design in motion (perfect physical balance would cause the parts to stabilize); but there should be no imbalance in the visual weights and the overall composition should have both visual unity and good design.

Changes are usually gradual and often seem to be on a minute scale. Many inventions were created seemingly by several unrelated minds work-

Flowers and Foliage

21 BIRD MOBILE (Photo by James Swan)

ing in the same direction, driven by the same stimulus. Who did invent the typewriter? It is often the one with the productive connections or know-how who receives the publicity and acclaim and is credited with the invention. But, within the framework of a smaller scale, we can find true creativity and personal expression in one's choices, selections, techniques, approaches, and philosophy.

Thus, for true enjoyment, knowledge is important, exposure is doubly important, and an open mind that is receptive to something which may have been presented in a new or slightly diversified form or variation is essential. Mrs. Osa Mae Barton, twenty-first President of the National Council of State Garden Clubs, Inc., once stated: "New ideas have been called a form of madness which is the salt that keeps us from decay."

And how can you recognize or appreciate subtle variations or new devices if you do not have some knowledge of that which came before?

Thus true enjoyment must be based upon some degree of knowledge and a spirit of appreciation, whether the artist utilizes paint and canvas or plant material and a container as his chosen medium. As with all artistic experiences, the more you can put into your viewing of flower arrangements, the more you can enjoy them.

SECTION II
How to Create the Flower Arrangements of Today

1 Design

In the past few years there has been a great resurgence of interest in the arts. Today, for the most part, we have plenty of everything, except possibly time. With an abundance of material things, selectivity and aesthetics play an even greater role in our lives.

The beauty that nature sets before us requires selection and discrimination when removed from its original setting. Colors which blend together harmoniously under a clear blue sky or in a sheltered spot in the garden require a faculty of judgment in their placement and combination indoors within a man-made setting.

Design, like manners, is everywhere, but that does not mean that all types are "good." Any time you pick and use plant material in any type of container you are creating a design, be it good or bad, because design is, of course, conscious organization.

Too much of our lives is based upon automatic responses, like buttoning a button, zipping a zipper, or frying an egg. We need the opportunity for emotional and aesthetic release offered in thoughtful self-expression and creative design. This applies not only to flower arranging but to all other activities in our lives.

There are several creative things which can be done with cut flowers. A single cut specimen—a lovely bud or flower or branch—placed casually by itself in a narrow-mouthed vase can be a thing of simple beauty. This casual placement and combination of flower and container emphasizes the horticultural qualities of the plant material, and is similar in effect to the Japanese Chabana (or "uncontrived" tea ceremony arrangement), although its design qualities are incidental.

The casual placement of a bunch of flowers in a vase can also be charming, as in the tulips in plate 22. Care must be taken to avoid crowding a bouquet, however, because this detracts from the individual qualities of each bloom, much as a crowd of people in an elevator obliterates the individual qualities of each person and the small boy in the rear may be completely obscured by the stout lady in the front.

Those interested in flower arranging have gone one step further and have created compositions using plant material according to the elements and principles of design. In order to do this, the glass frogs of grandma's day were replaced by oasis (a porous, waterlogged block used by florists) and by pinholders, heavy metal holders with needle-point pins upon which the individual flowers may be held in any desired angle and in any desired location.

For many years, the styles of arranging re-

22 **TULIPS** (Photo by Richard Hong)

Design

mained comparatively static. People did mass arrangements and line-mass arrangements in the form of ovals, triangles, crescents, and S-curves. Plate 23, an all-green arrangement, utilizes the foliage of house plants—sansevieria (snake plant), echeveria, and philodendron, in a simple triangular mass arrangement.

Plant material in these styles is manipulated into preconceived "designs." These were satisfactory in their way, but were often so stylized that flower arranging became a craft rather than a creative art.

The roots of our flower arranging of today lie not only in the mass arrangements of Europe, but in the line arrangements of the Orient. In plate 24, a classical Ikenobo Futakabu Shoka (a triangular design based on three main placements), there is "space for the birds to fly and the fish to swim" in the flow of plant material from one container and part of the design to the other. Willow knots painted burnt umber, pink protea, and variegated pink and green ti leaves were the plant materials used.

Within recent years, the mixing of two cultures and the freeflowing restlessness and rebellion of our era have caused a new surge of creativity to enter the field of arranging. Newer styles and approaches or attitudes have developed.

Modern creative free-form and free-style design uses any combination of materials, not just flowers alone. For example, in "Tick Tack Toe—Which Way Shall Pollution Go?" (plate 25), the metal which was used as an overall framework had holes drilled in it. Flowers inserted in aqua picks thus can be placed in any combination within the design. In plate 25, natural and bleached pampas grass were used in some picks to suggest the clouds of pollution, while crisp white geraniums were used in the others.

Plant material can include flowers in any phase of their development, from buds through seed pods, transitional materials, such as foliage from the garden or from house plants, and branches or vines, in any combination.

In flower arranging, a great awareness of the beauty in nature is constantly with us. But beauty alone cannot create a good design. Regardless of your approach, the elements and principles of design remain intact, although their emphasis and application will differ from time to time. The new designs of today, however, stress three things:

23 ALL FOLIAGE (Photo by Alwood Harvey)

1. LINE, which is the structural definition or bones of an arrangement. Strong, clean, uncluttered decisive line is basic. Line may be naturalistic or stylized, geometric or amorphic, but it is the structural essence of a design. Some line possibilities are shown in plate 26.

The plant material added to your basic line

44   *Flowers and Foliage*

24 DIVIDED SHOKA (Photo by Alwood Harvey)

25 TICK TACK TOE—WHICH WAY SHALL POLLUTION GO? (Photo by James Swan)

may be framed by line, may follow the linear pattern established, or may be in opposition to the established line (like a flying buttress).

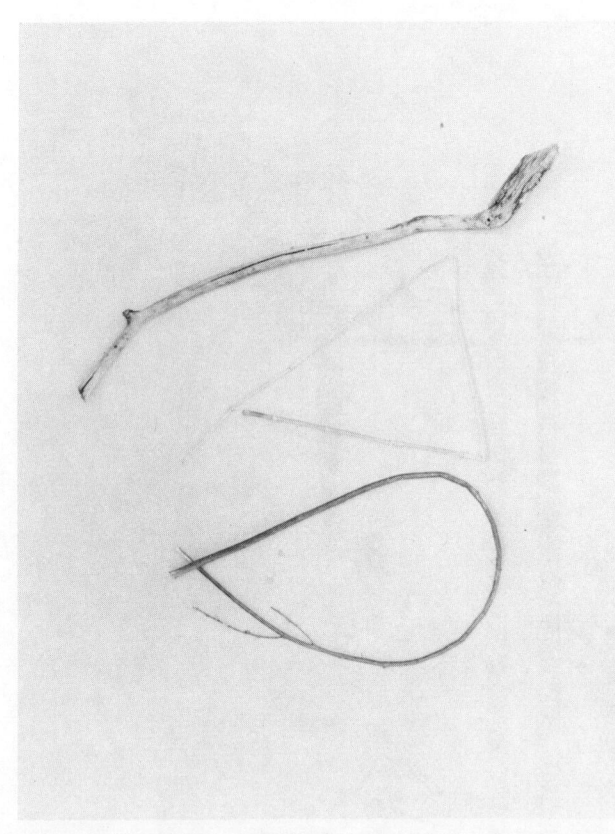

26 LINES (Photo by Alwood Harvey)

In plate 27, the bare bones of two strong crossing lines are all that is needed to express lightning, and the addition of anything else would be superfluous. Peeled willow branches were inverted to create dynamic tension and were inserted on the lip of a simple black ceramic pillar vase; a circular cutting board sprayed black forms the base.

2. SPACE RELATIONSHIPS are the interplay of solids and voids, scale and proportion. The less material you use, the more each item will register and the more you will need to know about both plant material and design. The spaces you leave empty in a good design are perhaps more important than the spaces you fill.

Clean simplicity is very deceptive. It is difficult to achieve without discipline and is the result of a high degree of sophistication and knowledge of both design and mechanics in its seemingly casual placement. Everything used, every flower and leaf and stem, must contribute to the overall design in the spaces filled or in the voids created.

In plate 28, two torch gingers and two pieces of sansevieria were placed in a pinholder in a modern ceramic container made by Connie Kemble. The strong horizontal line of the weathered wood, which balances on the container, forms an interesting spatial relationship.

3. TEXTURAL RICHNESS adds greatly to optical and tactile enjoyment. There is a wealth of textures available in nature, from velvet (as in mullein and cat-tails—both weeds) to satin (as in rose petals) to lace (Queen Anne's lace, a weed; parsley, a vegetable; hydrangea, a flower) to leathery (shrubs such as leucothoe, magnolia) to prickly (zucchini foliage, rex begonia).

There has always been a close affinity between the container and the composition. New materials such as plastics and metals, as well as modern pottery and weathered wood, all can play an important part. Pottery, china, glass, and fabrics also have a great range of textures.

Surfaces in flower arrangements need not be stark and sterile, but embellishments must have a *raison d'etre*. Variety and compatibility of textures enhance a design. Texture is also affected by light which, in turn, affects color.

"In the Oriental Manner," plate 29, utilizes seed pods of the gingerbread palm (for the *shin* or main line), bright orange umbellatum lilies (for the *soe* or secondary line), and a combination of both with lily foliage (for the *tai* or tertiary line) in a low bronze usubata on a grand piano. The texture and colors of the plant material, both fresh and dried, add greatly to the distinctive quality of this blue ribbon arrangement.

Flower arranging is done in a highly perishable medium and is perhaps the only art which goes from conception to execution to final evaluation and enjoyment within a matter of hours. Thus, a knowledge of conditioning and preserving the plant material, as well as maintaining the design with good mechanics, is of great importance. This knowledge becomes an integral factor in the overall design, in which techniques should be neither

27 LIGHTNING (Photo by Alwood Harvey)

28 **SPACE AND FORM** (Photo by James Swan)

29 IN THE ORIENTAL MANNER (Photo by Alwood Harvey)

30 **FLYING TRAPEZE** (Photo by George E. Ernst)

blatantly exposed nor coyly hidden, but part of the overall structure.

The use of new materials, plastics, metals, exotic tropicals, *et cetera,* are all interesting, but can only contribute their physical elements to a design. Eye-catching and shock techniques cannot of themselves create a good design. A strong, clean design and a fresh creative approach are the important considerations.

In any case, a good work of art has impact. This is more than a mere formula; it is the sum total of completion in a creative design, and the trained eye will respond to it as the trained ear will respond to a singer awarded a standing ovation.

In plate 30, absolute Spartan simplicity of line and placement adds to the dynamic tension as a small audience of three calla lilies and two yucca leaves look up at the "Flying Trapeze" of two cantilevered black V-forms of copper soldered to a black copper pipe. The calla lily heads were inserted into aqua picks.

Art cannot be separated from the play of intellect upon the subjective and the materials at its command. The objective materials of television, such as wave lengths, were present in the world of Archimedes, but the subjective materials were absent, and thus he could not possibly have devised television in his day. Cellini, if living today, would probably be creating masterpieces in platinum or perhaps aluminum (after all, we are off the gold standard) or even plastics; for he was able to use the subjective controls of his craft. The stars, the moon, and outer space existed in Galileo's era, but man lacked the means to explore them.

The artist, the flower arranger, the common man, must thus think in terms of materials and their uses and be restrained by their limitations. Painters can combine flowers of any season in their pictures, but flower arrangers must use what is available in the market or garden.

Thus, what is typical and intrinsically right for us in any time or particular medium may be intrinsically wrong in another. We cannot copy the past, although we can learn from it, nor can we anticipate the future. Colonial flower arrangers did not have our hybrids, clones, and cultivars —nor do we have the new varieties of tomorrow.

With this in mind, we are still involved in the equally important factors of knowing how and being able. When a craft evolves into the dignity of an art, objective materials must be employed to embody subtle artistic effects, both spiritual and utilitarian. This can only come about through conscious effort and deliberate thought.

Each person's creative effort must do its share of floundering as it develops, for creating is not a passive act. Books, museums, shows, lectures, and other arts are all helpful tools and sources of information and inspiration; but they do not take the place of actual personal experience. It is easier but less satisfactory to copy things which

Design 51

31 AS YOU LIKE IT by Nanette Gail Fields
(Photo by Alwood Harvey)

32 RED SAILS IN THE SUNSET by Nanette Gail Fields (Photo by George E. Ernst)

Design

custom declares safe. But in today's designs, one idea suggests another and the possibilities are unlimited, not stereotyped.

The clipped white pine and yellow roses in plate 31, all fresh plant material, form a modified traditional crescent in a small black salad bowl in this charming blue ribbon arrangement by Nanette Gail Fields, who was eleven when she created it. The title was "As You Like It" and this is what she liked—at that time.

Today taste is eclectic and indicative of one's personality. What you use in your home and choose to combine is limited only by your preferences and aesthetics, not dictated by formula or arbitrary rules. More and more people today realize that an acceptance and understanding of change is essential if work in any medium is to go forward, not remain static.

The selective pruning and sensitive handling of two branches of horse chestnut and the gladioli in plate 32 shows the development of Nanette Gail Fields' talents and technique. "Red Sails in the Sunset" was created when she was fourteen years old and was exhibited, but not in competition, at the International Flower Show in New York in a high school gardeners' invitation section.

No artist can always create masterpieces. Conversely, neither can any work of art be achieved without trying, regardless of the medium employed. Nor does success in one area, such as watercolor painting, guarantee success in another, such as ceramics, until the fundamental mechanics of that particular technique are explored and mastered. The important thing for all of us to remember is that the process of creating, the spirit of adventure and learning through experimentation, is every bit as important as the final result.

In flower arranging, as in everything else, if your early achievements are less than you might wish, re-evaluate your approach and try again. Plant material is both relatively inexpensive and perishable. No mistake is, therefore, either permanent or costly. Any flower arrangement can bring color, warmth, and sparkle to your home, but today's arrangements can be both a mental stimulus and a challenge as well. Once you try one you will find it much more satisfactory than a bunch of flowers merely tossed into a vase, particularly if you appreciate flowers.

There is so much you can learn from looking at the natural curves of each piece of plant material. No two are alike; there is such infinite variety. Some flowers look up, some look down, some are more interesting in profile. All of these physical characteristics can add interest and variety to your design.

Start with the materials you find at hand and experiment. For example, green is the predominant color in nature, the expected and accepted one. Thus, by eliminating green from a composition, and using red or mahogany-colored foliage, you can obtain an off-beat effect.

The musical violinist figurine in plate 33 was used as the central linear accent for a holiday arrangement in which green-bronze foliage and the red stems of the Joe Hayden begonia (from my house plant) and the green-gold color of the Duchess chrysanthemum add an interesting color quality to a simple composition. The flowers were placed in a round cup-pinholder.

Don't start with a completely preconceived design—it won't work, or if it does, it will be too contrived. Do each step and refine your design as it goes along. Commonplace, mundane things handled in a distinctive fashion can create unusual effects; *e.g.,* creating "grapes" with walnuts or Brussels sprouts, or bending "green" cat-tails into curves before they dry. Considerable knowledge of horticulture is often developed in trying to pick the right material for the space, the form, and the texture desired. It is also interesting to note that plant material indigenous to one area may be considered quite exotic in another.

Reversing a line will change its direction; inverting a line or branch redistributes its feeling of weight. Crossing vertical and parallel lines will produce a stronger pattern and more dominant areas.

In plate 34, all dry material was used for a Halloween centerpiece by Melinda Sue Fields, who was fifteen years old at the time. The bare "tree" is a root, washed, painted black, and placed in a pinholder upside-down. The "grapes" are acorns which were wired together; one bunch was placed on either side of the composition.

The words "flower" and "line" are both ab-

54 *Flowers and Foliage*

33 MUSICAL VIOLINIST (Photo by James Swan)

Design

34 HALLOWEEN by Melinda Sue Fields (Photo by Alwood Harvey)

stractions as they appear in a sentence. They become concrete again when used in application to a particular thing—in a painting or in a flower arrangement. We abstract a thing by imaginatively placing it outside its usual connections. This can best be done after skill has been developed with mechanics, but skill with ideas and an open mind are a prerequisite to skill with things. A truly practical and creative person must be able to abstract ideas into concrete situations to get them to work.

A creative idea usually develops gradually from its initial inspiration. If the physical materials are at hand, the arranger could try out an idea while it is fresh in the mind. Sometimes it will take shape with the first attempt, but often substitution of materials can improve a composition. Try several combinations of plant material to see which achieves the most effective result: the flat shiny form of a red anthurium, the round open form of a rubrum lily, or the solid red form of a red peony.

Viewing your arrangement from a distance often helps you see it in its entirety. If space does not permit this, try viewing it through the wrong end of a pair of binoculars, thus reducing it to a miniature. If a polaroid camera is available, take a picture of it; often seeing it in black and white (without the distractions of color) will show you the strong or weak points of your design. Another good technique for self-evaluation is to analyze your arrangement in front of a mirror; this will help you spot flaws in balance.

But perhaps the best and simplest method for evaluating your arrangement is to go away from it for a while and then come back to it. You know what you have been trying to do and it is hard to separate this from what you have done without the perspective of time.

Flower arranging, as an art, follows the same patterns and is influenced by the same trends and changes as other arts, although it often reflects these trends later rather than simultaneously. Perhaps this is because flower arranging touches upon the art of the potter for containers, the art of the sculptor for figurines, the art of the carpenter for bases, the art of the weaver for background fabrics, the skill of the botanist for plant material, the world of the chemist for treating and preserving dried material, the art of the photographer for reproduction. We need many arts for sampling and placing our chosen medium in proper perspective, with minute attention to its various component details.

Thus, what you do and how you do it are all part of your basic philosophy and makeup. Flower arranging should be fun, a source of relaxation, enjoyment, and pleasure. I have often said this to my students and more than once it has snapped back at me, particularly when I have been trying to get exhibitors for a flower show—for what may be sheer enjoyment at one time may not be at other times!

But there are certain essentials in the creation of every flower arrangement:

1. A mind ready to grapple with the problem.
2. Plant material suitable to your design concept.
3. A container.
4. Mechanics to hold your plant materials in their designated design.
5. A place in which to put the completed arrangement, whether it is in a show or at home.

2
Plant Material to Grow

One of the best ways to "find" distinctive plant material is to become a horticulturist and grow it yourself. However, a perceptive eye is important so that you will recognize the possibilities to be found in the interesting forms and various stages of the life cycle of most plants, flowers, vegetables, and trees, from bud through seed pod, as our seasons progress through the year.

The delicate light green tones of rhubarb flowers in plate 35 combined with the red rhubarb stalks and the dark green rhubarb foliage were used in a cup-pinholder on a black wooden base with several pieces of decorative wood that had been nailed and glued together to form a composition to illustrate some of the everyday possibilities which can be found around us.

We all recognize the beauty of the apple blossom; the cherry blossom is world famous. But do we ever think of utilizing the blossom of the rhubarb, the flower of onions? We know the beauty of the wisteria vine, but what about the Virginia creeper? We know the beauty of ti leaves, pothos, galax, rex begonias, but what about the beauty of the castor bean (in leaf, in flower, and in seed pod), of zucchini foliage, of corn shucks and tassels?

Nature has endowed us with an infinite variety of ever-changing colors, textures, lines, patterns, and forms. The observant arranger can be discriminating in the choice of materials and will enjoy organizing these elements to create beauty and interesting designs. This chapter will cover only a few recommended varieties. Each of you can find many, many more.

Trees

A branch is one pattern when dormant, another when it is partially covered with budding foliage, still another when the leaves are mature. A budding branch, incidentally, generally has more linear interest than a fully developed one whose pattern is obscured by foliage. And a gnarled or jagged branch can often be an exciting line structure.

"Spring," plate 36, utilizes freesia and the budding branches of a maple in a basic three-line Ikenobo Shoka pattern. The color of the container, black, brown, and tan, has the earthy quality of early spring; it is of Japanese origin.

"Fall," plate 37, in contrast, utilizes crab apple branches and yellow fall chrysanthemums in an Ikenobo divided Shoka pattern. In this case, the container is a simple homemade one of two square cup-pinholders and their framework support.

There is no such thing as having *nothing* with

Flowers and Foliage

interesting and hardy plant which will grow readily, as does the corkscrew willow, if it is provided with sufficient moisture. As the branches grow, they flatten into broad curving lines which circle around. In early spring they are covered with gray pussy willow blooms.

Bamboo, fan-tail willow, dried okra pods, and crocus were used in the Gendai (or modern) Rikka in plate 39 in a modern ceramic container by Estelle Halper. Every well-planned arrangement should have good front to back or radial depth (as much as is practical in the location in which it will be placed). This is difficult to show in a picture; for this reason, in plate 40, this arrangement was photographed in profile as well.

Vegetables

In the vegetable garden there are innumerable

35 RHUBARB (Photo by George E. Ernst)

which to work if you are a creative, perceptive person. In "Winter," plate 38, Nanette Gail Fields used bare branches, juniper, and andromeda, all commonplace evergreens and branches from our foundation plantings, with a deer figurine. The plant material was placed in a cup-pinholder on a natural burl base. She was thirteen when she created this lovely winter composition.

Many new plants have become available within recent years. The fan-tail willow from Japan is an

36 SPRING (Photo by James Swan)

37 FALL (Photo by James Swan)

38 **WINTER by Nanette Gail Fields (Photo by Alwood Harvey)**

39 **BAMBOO AND FAN-TAIL WILLOW** (Photo by James Swan)

40 Profile of plate 39 (Photo by James Swan)

plants which are easy to grow, edible, and have exciting or challenging forms.

The Egyptian tree onion produces onion sets on top of its stems. The stems also curve, bend, and twist in interesting patterns. In plate 41, four tree onions and five pieces of self-foliage were combined with an allium in a low kidney-shaped Haeger container.

Most alliums (onions) have starry, ball-like flowers which are beautiful blooms but have the added feature of drying well if they are permitted to go to seed.

Flowering kale or cabbage, *Brassica oleracea*, can be grown from seed in a sunny garden. One cut plant makes a handsome dominance in any arrangement. The color range is from white, pink, or deep red through green. Some are ruffled, while others are heavily curled and fringed.

Nature also produces some unusual seed pods, often striking in form, such as martynia. This looks somewhat like a large insect when it dries and opens. It may be grown in the vegetable garden purely for picking purposes.

Okra, in addition to being a useful vegetable, also provides an interesting design form. Dried okra stalks and seed pods form the basis of the arrangement in plate 42 in a long, low, flat-textured ceramic container. Some of the seed pods were split open to create a flower form in the design.

There are also a number of interesting forms of gourds, as well as squash (*e.g.,* crook-neck squash, Turk's-cap squash) which have great design possibilities for arrangers.

Two crook-neck squash and weathered wood with sansevieria, miniature pineapples, and Brus-

Plant Material to Grow

sels sprouts wired together as cascading grapes were used to create a feeling of "Fall Bounty" (plate 43). The entire composition was in shades of green, beige, and browns, not the usual fall colors, but effective, nevertheless, in this simple line-mass composition. (The use of a wooden tooth pick is a great aid in anchoring fruit and vegetables to each other.)

"Soup de Jour," a vegetable mobile in plate 44, was designed for a lecture. It was constructed with needle and embroidery thread. All of the vegetables were in a very firm under-ripe stage; this, incidentally, gave great color unity to the design, for the tonal quality ranged in an analogous run from dark blue-green cucumbers, zucchini, and peppers through the lighter tones of the yellow-green tomatoes and green-gold carrots. A design of this type can lack a cohesive quality unless there is a deliberate unity of form and color.

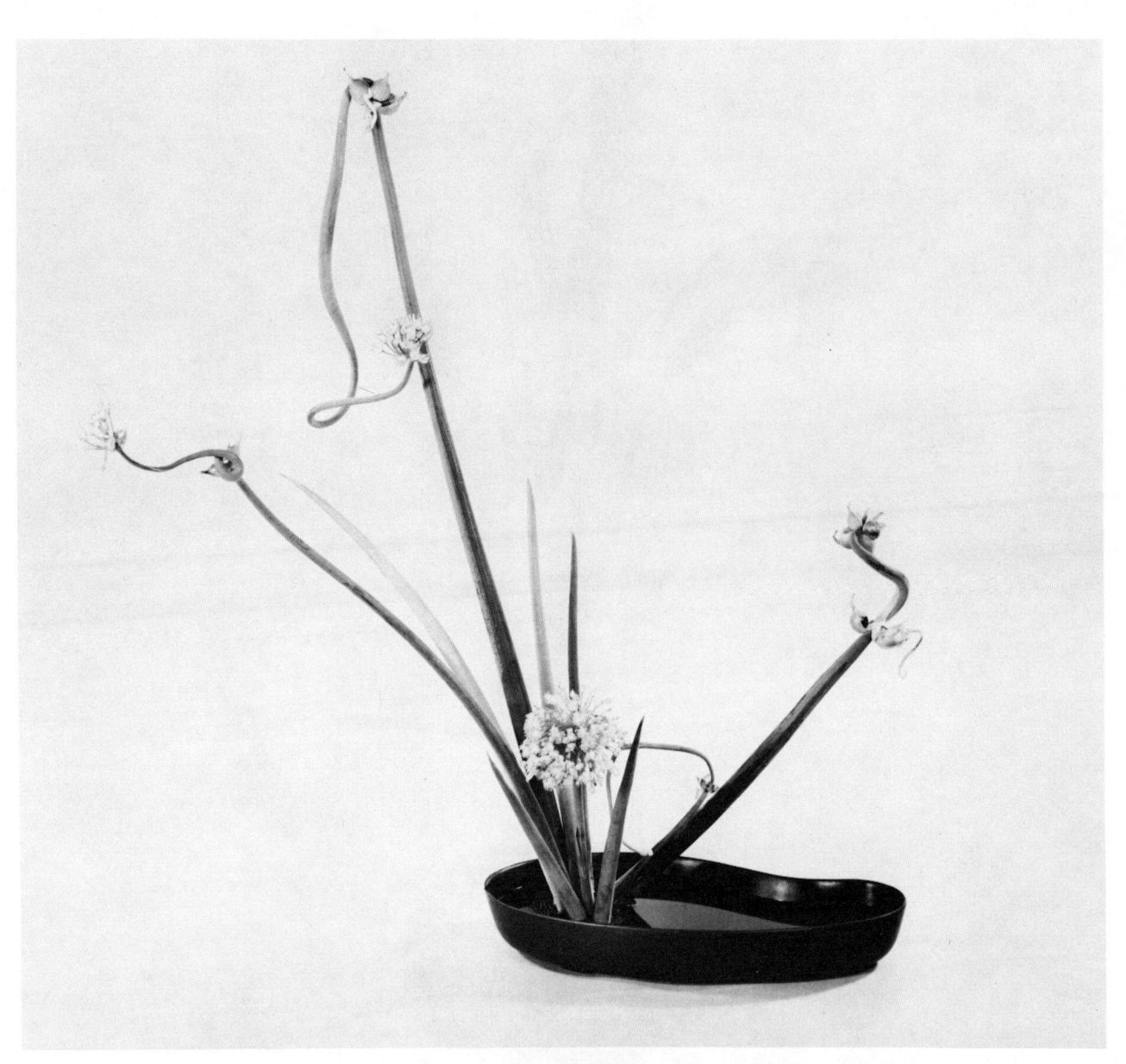

41 **EGYPTIAN TREE ONIONS** (Photo by James Swan)

42 OKRA (Photo by James Swan)

THE LUTE PLAYER (Photo by James Forney)

MUSICAL VIOLINIST (Photo by James Swan)

43 FALL BOUNTY (Photo by Bill Sevecke)

44 SOUP DE JOUR (Photo by Alwood Harvey)

Pot Plants

Within the *Cyperaceae* family (some are called papyrus) there are interesting forms which produce green starry flower-like forms on top of long, straight stems. This green papyrus was used with green ti leaves, green gladioli, and bamboo in plate 45 in a cup-pinholder elevated on a black twist of iron to create "Modern Music," a blue ribbon winner.

Euphorbia pedilanthus (devil's claw) has a tall, zigzag stem. In certain stages of its development it becomes semidormant and loses its foliage. It is a hardy, easily grown plant.

A flat cactus, *Cryptocereus anthonyanus,* looks like a wide rickrack braid. It blooms with a large, fragrant, water-lily type of white flower, but is grown primarily for foliage. It, too, is a hardy pot plant; like most succulents, it is a heavy feeder and should be fertilized monthly for best leaf development and substance.

In "The Sea," plate 46, rickrack cactus and white lilies were combined with a sea fan and an interesting piece of driftwood that resembled a wave.

Night-blooming cereus has long stems and leathery leaves, but grows quite large as the plant matures. The flower, which opens at night, is a striking sight (although since it lasts but one evening, it is not useful for the arranger). From about 9 p.m. through 2 a.m. it opens its stunning white petals as you watch it; its odor is sweet but somewhat cloying. Many people have a midnight party just to watch the flower unfold. It forms the flower on the side of a leaf, as do many other cacti and succulents.

Satiny white calla lilies contrast effectively with the leathery leaves from a night-blooming cereus in plate 47. They were used in a blue ribbon arrangement in a radiating design by Melinda Sue Fields, who was fifteen at the time. The modern ceramic vase is by Ginnie Gilson.

In plate 48, shrimp-plant, *Beloperone guttata,* a vining pot-plant which has interesting shrimp-colored pink flowers, was combined with a few pieces of weathered wood for both design emphasis and structural stability. A cup-pinholder contains the necessary water.

Other pot plants which have possibilities for the arranger are bromeliads, whose leaves are tough and durable, some having striped patterns; marantha plants, whose foliage has bizarre coloring; dieffenbachia, which has large spotted or striped leaves; pandanus, which has long strap fo-

Plant Material to Grow 67

45 MODERN MUSIC (Photo by Bill Sevecke)

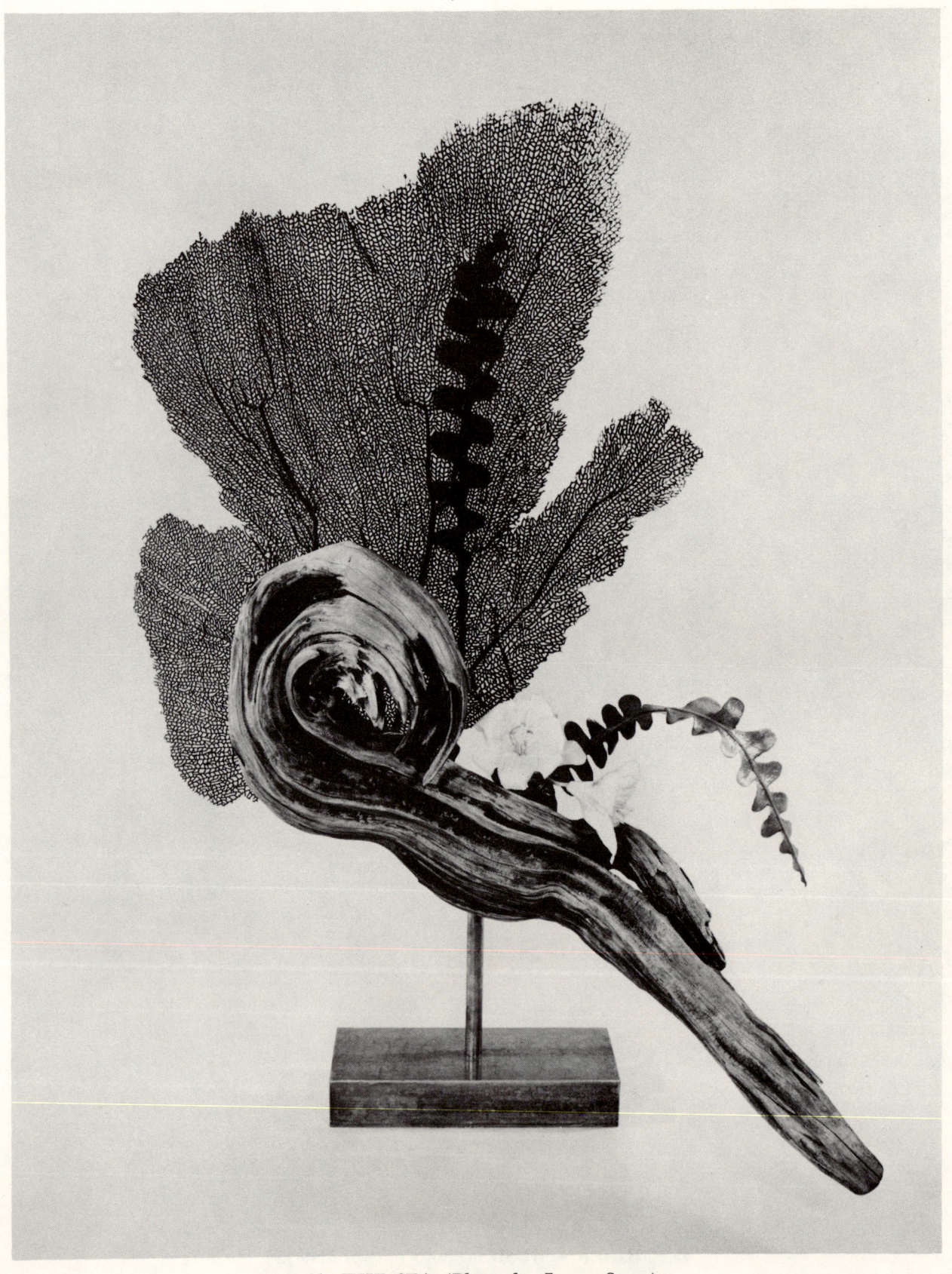

46 THE SEA (Photo by James Swan)

47 NIGHT-BLOOMING CEREUS by Melinda Sue Fields (Photo by George E. Ernst)

49 POT PLANT FOLIAGE (Photo by Alwood Harvey)

48 SHRIMP-PLANT AND WOOD (Photo by James Swan)

50 HOSTA, PHLOX, AND LARCH (Photo by James Swan)

Plant Material to Grow

liage, both serrated and smooth; monstera and philodendron, with many interesting cut leaves of a large size; rex begonia, offering great variations of color, pattern, and texture; and anthurium and alocasia.

Plate 49 shows many types. Running clockwise they are: ti leaf, Joe Hayden begonia, anthurium leaf, fish-tail palm, zebra plant, night-blooming cereus, rickrack cactus, angelwing begonia, Swiss cheese philodendron—all from my pot plants.

Don't overlook the possibilities of using a root structure if a pot plant dies; after you shake off the soil, an interesting form may be found which can be washed, bleached, or spray painted. It can become an unusual component part of a design, particularly if used in an inverted position with the trunk stem down and the hairy roots up, as in plate 34.

Garden Plants

Two hardy and invaluable perennial garden foliage plants are saxifrage, which has a strong leathery foliage, and the many varieties of hosta, which range from yellow-green through blue-green and variegated varieties with from small to large leaves.

In plate 50, two variegated hosta leaves were used with the spiky violet hosta flower, Queen Anne's lace, pink phlox, and larch branches. Larch, incidentally, is a particularly effective type of evergreen to use because it is in such good scale and proportion to the average arrangement that it does not overpower it.

Saxifrage leaves are used in plate 51 with forsythia branches which had lost most of their foliage in the late fall, one cat-tail, one blue hydrangea, and some evergreen taxus cuttings in a Gendai Rikka. The container is a handsome Japanese ceramic.

Caladium, too, has striking variegated foliage and a wide color range, but is of a weaker texture. Bulbs must be lifted from the garden in the fall in most parts of the country.

The circular rosette forms of many succulents are excellent additions to creative designs; and a common variety, hen-and-chickens, is a hardy rock-garden staple, available in many sizes and color variations. Since they do not have a natural stem, for they grow low on the ground, they may be wired to a branch or stem of your own composition. They will keep quite well without water for a reasonable length of time and may be re-rooted later in sandy soil.

Some of the more exotic varieties of cacti and succulents may also be grown as pot plants. Many compact forms belong to the *Crassulaceae* family, some are aloes, others are kalanchoes, which have lovely form and texture, some are echeveria, which are often found in silvery, bronze, or violet tones. They range from small to large varieties.

A large aloe, night-blooming cereus, and sansevieria from three house plants were combined with the sculptured boxer I made some years ago, because the strength, virility, and textures of these materials were compatible for "Knock-out Punch" (plate 52), a blue ribbon winner.

Another example of plant material that we all admire is the beautiful forms and colors of hemerocallis (day lily) when they are in bloom. Varieties range in color from the common orange and yellow of the native bloom to hybrids of pale cream, through deep bronze and maroon tones. Although each flower lasts for but a day, hence the common name, the stalk bears a profusion of buds which open in sequence. This hardy perennial is an asset to every garden. The stalks may be used in flower arrangements as a handsome line material when the buds are barely formed. Later, the stalks bearing seed pods create a different effect, equally useful for line.

Bright orange native hemerocallis were used with two nepenthes leaves from a house plant in plate 53, in a modern bubbly-textured ceramic container by Estelle Halper. The two cat-tails appear to radiate out of the vase; they were curved while still fresh and green, being placed between the webs of a terrace chair and allowed to dry there. (When the seed heads of cat-tails or pampas grass are sprayed either with clear aerosol shellac or with hair spray, they will keep indefinitely without fuzzing-out.) Basket-weaving willow from a crafts shop was soaked and then bent into sweeping curves. This arrangement was designed for a lecture to illustrate "Swing Your Partner," and the round wooden tray, turned upside down, forms the dance floor base. The use

51 SAXIFRAGE AND HYDRANGEA (Photo by James Swan)

Plant Material to Grow 73

52 KNOCK-OUT PUNCH (Photo by Bill Sevecke)

53 **SWING YOUR PARTNER** (Photo by James Swan)

Plant Material to Grow 75

54 FASCIATED MULLEIN AND WOOD (Photo by James Swan)

of various plant elements in pairs also helps to interpret the theme.

If tulips, Siberian iris, and poppies are left to go to seed, they form a lovely cream-colored pod which dries on the long stem. Rose hips, too, are an interesting form and remain a bright red as the seed develops within.

Field and Roadside Plants

The blossom spike of dock, a common weed, has great beauty when stripped of its foliage and can be used for line material in its fresh green stage. In late summer, it turns a beautiful russet brown, handsome for dried arrangements.

Mullein is another plant which has innumerable phases and possibilities. Its gray-green furry foliage in spring and summer is lovely; in the fall, long spiky seed pods form. Occasionally they can be found fasciated. These enlarged and flattened deformations usually occur when the mullein, which has been grown at the roadside, is sprayed by the highway department with a weedkiller or defoliant. Five pieces of dried fasciated mullein in a cup-pinholder and some weathered wood were used to create the composition in plate 54.

We are all familiar with the rich red color of sumac berries in the autumn; but have you ever thought of using them in the summer months when they are a fresh chartreuse?

55 PINGPONG, ANYONE? (Photo by James Swan)

Plant Material to Grow

Certain vines (honeysuckle, wisteria, Virginia creeper, grape, ampelopsis) can be cut while fresh and flexible, then stripped of their bark and foliage to reveal a pale green color which dries to a creamy tone. When stripped of their cambium layer, they dry quite quickly. These vines may be bent, knotted, or tied to create unusual and interesting rhythmic lines. They can be wrapped around a bottle, jar, or cone to create a spiral, then tied to hold them in place while they dry. They can also be looped or twisted into innumerable shapes created by placing nails in a sheet of plywood and bending the vines around them.

They can also be used without stripping the bark, and will then dry a dark brown which contrasts nicely with the peeled vines.

If the vines are not flexible enough, or if they have already dried and you wish to rebend them, they may be soaked or boiled to soften them. Vines are usually defoliated because their foliage tends to obscure their linear pattern and quality.

Two Virginia creeper vines, one natural, one peeled, were boiled in a large pot to soften them and then bent into loops for plate 55. Two pingpong balls were punctured with an ice pick and then pressed over the ends of the vines; one had previously been sprayed black, one was left in its natural color for variety. The other end of the vines was inserted into a pinholder in a textured ceramic pot by Estelle Halper. The ends with the pingpong balls were allowed to rest on the table and on the base. Two bright red spikes of gladiolus were inserted into the pinholder, back to back, so that the arrangement, which is completely freestanding, may be viewed from any side. This modern amorphic freestyle composition, suitable for a coffee table, could be titled "Let's Have a Ball" or "Pingpong, Anyone?" There is no reason flower arranging cannot express a bit of humor or whimsy.

3
Forcing Shrubs and Trees

Almost any tree or shrub that blooms or leafs out in early spring can be forced into bloom earlier. The flower buds of all spring-blooming shrubs are formed in the fall. After a period of about six weeks of cold weather with alternate freezing or low temperatures and milder thaws, the buds are chemically ready to break dormancy and grow when warmth and moisture are supplied.

Some branches will force in a relatively short period of time—pussy willow in a matter of days, forsythia in about a week to ten days; other varieties may take longer. The length of time needed for forcing will vary with the species chosen and the proximity of its normal flowering period.

Select for forcing branches which have larger, fatter buds on younger shoots and branches which have interesting lines, curves, or angles. To avoid subsequent disease or insect damage when removing branches from your trees or bushes, use a pruning shears to obtain a clean flush cut, for this will heal over rapidly.

Mash or shred the cut end of the stem to encourage water intake. Then moisten the buds by soaking the branches overnight in tepid water in a bath tub or wash tub. If a suitable container for this deep water immersion is unavailable, cover the branches with layers of wet burlap.

After overnight soaking, place the crushed ends of the branches in deep water, in pails or old cider jugs, in a temperate location of about 60° to 65° and out of direct sunlight or air currents and drafts while the buds develop. A piece of charcoal in the water will help prevent it from spoiling. Change the water about once each week until the buds have developed.

The lilacs in plate 56 were forced and then combined with white pine and semi-dormant deciduous branches in a casual, airy Nageire style arrangement in the modern ceramic container by Ginnie Gilson.

In plate 57, both the lilacs and the pussy willow were forced by Nanette Gail Fields, and then combined with driftwood and a pair of mallards to create the feeling of spring in her line-mass composition, created when she was fifteen. Pussy willow, incidentally, forces very quickly; lilacs take a longer period of time.

A dormant branch may be held over for subsequent use later in the spring if you wrap it loosely in cloth and place it in your home freezer. When you wish to break the dormancy, follow the procedure for freshly cut branches, starting with overnight soaking, as previously indicated.

In plate 58, the deciduous spiraea was held back, rather than forced, so that it was covered with tiny green new buds just breaking their

Forcing Shrubs and Trees 79

56 NAGEIRE OF LILAC AND PINE (Photo by George E. Ernst)

57 **PUSSY WILLOW AND LILAC** by Nanette Gail Fields (Photo by George E. Ernst)

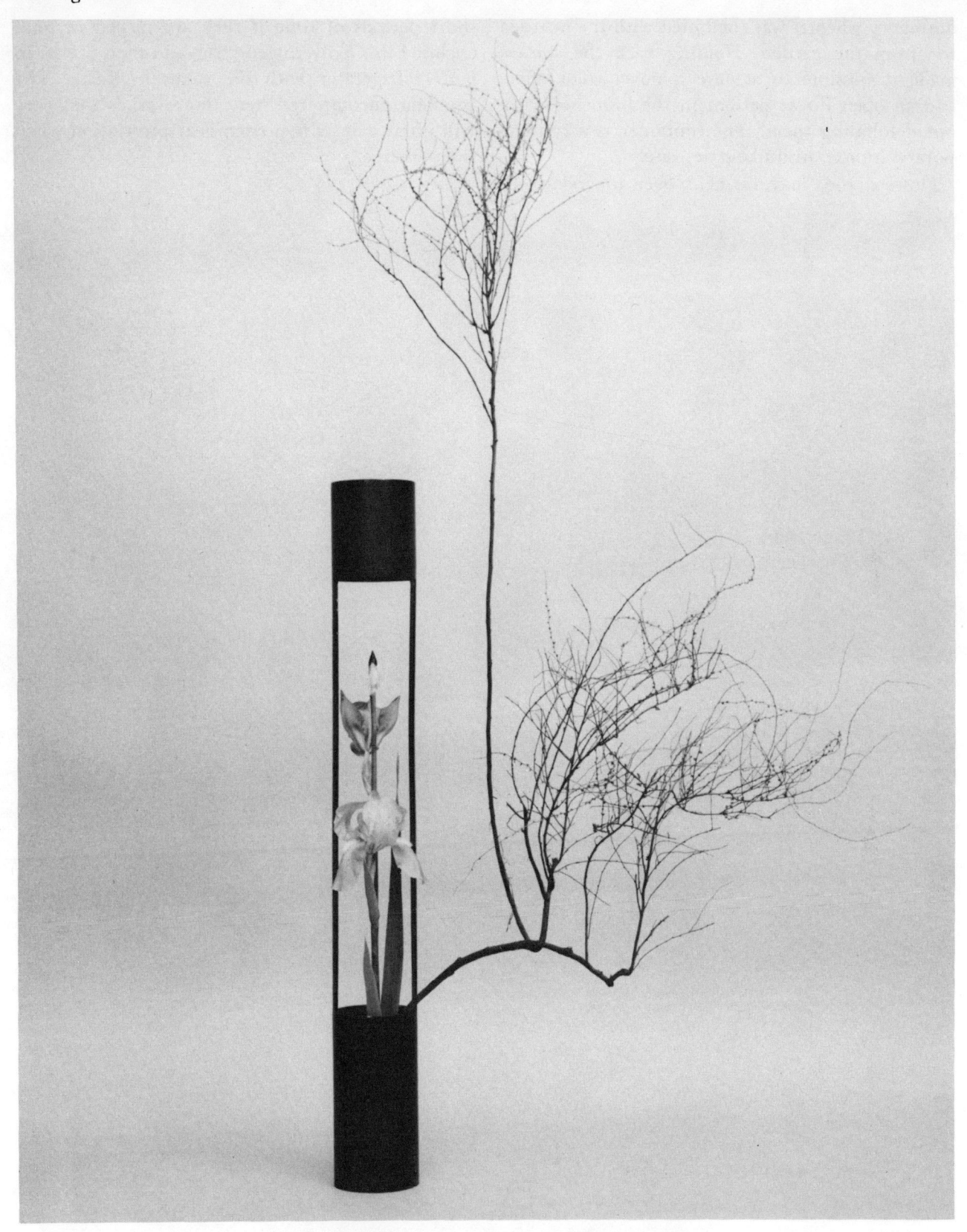

Forcing Shrubs and Trees

58 **NISHUIKE OF SPIREA AND IRIS** (Photo by George E. Ernst)

dormancy when it was combined with the bearded iris from the garden. Holding back the spiraea made it possible to achieve a novel color effect and an open linear pattern in the branches without defoliating them. The container is a contemporary bronze nishuike-style vase.

Flowers, too, may be held over for relatively short periods of time if they are picked in bud, enclosed in a polyethylene bag, and then placed in your refrigerator with the stems in water. The problem encountered here, however, is that they will often wilt or flop from heat prostration when they emerge.

4
Conditioning of Fresh Plant Material

Creative expression in any medium has been valued for the enjoyment it brings as well as for its end product. Flower arranging fits into this category particularly well as the materials used are perishable and transitory, but their use is all the more valuable because of this. A fresh flower arrangement never falls into the realm of dust collector or white elephant, but adds a dash of color and decorative warmth to home and shows alike.

Flower arrangements are here and then gone, but the enjoyment aroused in their creation can become part of a way of life, and will sharpen our perception to the fleeting beauty in the world around us, whether it is in a cloud, a garden flower, or a weed growing by the roadside. Flower arrangements appeal to our senses—scent, sight, touch.

Plant material purchased from the florist is always "conditioned," but plant material picked by the arranger in the house, garden, field, or side of the highway usually must be prepared before it can be used in an arrangement. There are, of course, some exceptions, for iris and day lilies may be used as soon as they have been picked, with no ill effects or premature wilting. Most plant material, however, needs special preparation before it can be used if you wish it to hold up in an arrangement.

The simplest technique for all plant material (including iris and day lilies) is to pick it early in the morning before the sun has dehydrated it, or in the early evening after the sun has set. It should then be placed in a deep container of water (a gallon cider jug is good) away from direct light or heat or draft for about 8 to 10 hours.

The interesting stems and strong vertical thrust of the pink peonies in plate 59, which had been conditioned overnight, add to the vertical quality of the black columnar ceramic vase. A piece of weathered wood anchored on the lip of the vase by means of its unpruned lateral contributes a diagonal accent to this modern freestyle composition.

Dahlias, poppies, zinnias, euphorbias, poinsettias, and other plants which exude a milky sap need to be seared with a direct flame from a match or candle; this clots the sap and prevents further bleeding. Then the stem should be immersed in deep water for conditioning. When recut to the proper length in an arrangement, the stems should be reburned, but repeating the deep water conditioning is not necessary.

84   *Flowers and Foliage*

The bright orange double hemerocallis used in plate 61 required no conditioning, but the night-blooming cereus was seared and then conditioned. The royal poinciana pods were pre-soaked in hot water and then bent into suitable curves for this "Study in Textures." The base is a brown cork hotplate and the dark brown clay container by Estelle Halper was partially covered with random bubbly beige and orange glaze.

A clean cut stem is important. You should cut with a sharp knife or snips and immediately place the plant material into water before the cells scar over. Many Japanese, who have a long tradi-

59 PEONIES AND WOOD (Photo by George E. Ernst)

The blue ceramic vase used in plate 60, with its unglazed bisque decoration, suggests the undulating quality of waves lapping against the beach. The two pieces of bent scrap metal sprayed beige help to create a frame of reference for the composition and reinforce the design motif of the container. They hook on the lip of one side and extend to a hole drilled in the other side. A twisted curl of cane weaving willow was inserted to add depth and pink garden dahlias add a final sunlit note to the overall composition.

60 DAHLIAS, CERAMIC, AND METAL (Photo by George E. Ernst)

61 **STUDY IN TEXTURES** (Photo by James Swan)

tion of flower arranging, cut their plant material under water to insure freshness. This is important both when conditioning and when arranging flowers.

The football chrysanthemum, a strong bronze hue, and the oak foliage which, touched by the first frost, turned a beautiful red and golden color, are a perfect foil for the strongly grained wooden container. Color, texture and line are all combined in plate 62. Chrysanthemums, incidentally, are an extremely long-lasting flower (sometimes staying fresh from two to three weeks), particularly when they have been cut and conditioned properly.

Many beginning arrangers dislike cutting off the long stems of flowers, but a shorter stem is a shorter distance for the water to travel via capillary action up the stem to keep the flower fresh. Thus, a short-stemmed flower has a better chance of achieving a long life than one with a long stem. This is true whether the flowers are loosely placed in a bouquet or arranged in a pinholder. And, of course, varying the stem lengths is important in creating good design.

Flowers from a pot plant are handled in the same manner as garden flowers. And, if you are a window-sill or greenhouse gardener you just may have flowers when others do not.

62 CHRYSANTHEMUM AND OAK (Photo by James Swan)

63 SHRIMP PLANT AND FLUTE PLAYER
(Photo by James Swan)

64 **BLAST OFF** (Photo by Alwood Harvey)

Conditioning of Fresh Plant Material

65 AFTER THE BOAT RACE (Photo by Bill Sevecke)

In plate 63, a few flowers from a shrimp plant, *Beloperone guttata,* and some weathered wood were combined with a beautiful wood carving of an oriental flute player. There is a very compatible quality in these delicate flowers and the sculptured girl in her flowing robe.

The stems of some flowers such as tulips and tritoma have a tendency to turn toward the light, even after they have been placed in an arrangement. Needless to say, this can often create serious design complications; using them on short stems, as in plate 64, can help to minimize this problem. In "Blast Off," a blue ribbon winner, the bent and partially defoliated forsythia branch takes off from the cup-pinholder, leaving in its wake the three bright red-orange tritoma and two ti leaves, one bent and one cut into long trailing strands. The entire arrangement was placed on an amorphic homemade metal construction which repeats the spatial voids and flow of the plant material.

The white calla lilies used for the table centerpiece in plate 65 required the special handling accorded all soft-stemmed bulbs such as amaryllis, daffodils, and tulips. After they were conditioned and re-cut to size for the arrangement, the bottom side of each stem was ringed with a strip of Band-aid clear tape to prevent it from splitting. (The base of the stem is never covered or the flower would be unable to receive its water supply.)

Pandanus foliage and a cup-pinholder in a homemade black boat complete the blue ribbon arrangement which was titled "After the Boat Race." The Dansk plates were black and white,

66 **PENTHOUSE GLAMOUR** (Photo by Bill Sevecke)

Conditioning of Fresh Plant Material 91

67 PI IN THE SKY (Photo by Alwood Harvey)

the napkins black Irish linen, and the cloth turquoise Irish linen.

Flowers are best utilized on individual stems and it is often a good idea to separate those in a spray, partly because they will then be more effective in the composition and partly because they will last longer when they do not have to compete with each other for a limited water supply obtained through one main stem. Another important point is to defoliate all leaves which will be under water, thus discouraging unpleasant bacterial growth.

It is a good idea to remove excess foliage up the stem of a flower for two additional reasons. Transpiration (water loss) continues through the leaves, and a cut flower thus may lose more water than it can receive. Also, deliberate placement of leaves on their own stems at desired locations will often clarify a design and is infinitely better than taking pot-luck with them where they have grown.

In Ikebana (Japanese flower arranging) there is one deceptively simple but beautiful design, an ishuike of iris, in which all iris flowers and their leaves are disassembled and then reassembled to create an idealized growth pattern, much as the ancient Greek sculptors carved the idealized forms of man with a physique infinitely superior to that of any living person.

In plate 66, three red carnations were used on rather short stems in three cup-pinholders; elevation was achieved with the scrap metal "container." This arrangement, subtitled "Penthouse Glamour," was exhibited at a New York State Annual Meeting where all of the arrangements, which were not in competition, depicted various phases of "Spotlight on New York." Plant material such as the red carnations and the green and variegated ti leaves added a note of formality, as did the white marble base. Carnation stems and foliage curls were used as accents.

Some arrangers like to add one or two drops of vinegar (acetic acid) to their water, some like to add one aspirin, or the commercial preparations which are available at your local florist's (such as Floralife). Actually, nothing takes the place of clean tepid water. Never use ice water, as it will shock a plant and cause the capillaries to contract.

If a flower appears prematurely wilted, it may be immersed (up to but not including the flower head) in rather hot water to revive it. This is often helpful to zinnias and roadside flowers. The neck of some flowers, such as African daisies, will often weaken overnight. Recutting the stem half an inch or so shorter will reopen the capillaries and revive the flower by permitting water to pass up the stem.

Some plant materials, such as hydrangeas, are particularly in need of a long deep-water bath, which may also include the flower head, to condition them properly.

The blue garden hydrangeas in plate 67 held up for several weeks after they had been conditioned. "Pi in the Sky," a blue ribbon arrangement, combined two hydrangeas, two pieces of yucca, and pampas grass stems bent and inserted at varying angles to add depth to the composition in an angular homemade metal container.

Your pinholder and container, needless to say, should always be clean. An old toothbrush will help remove any vegetative matter which may have become lodged on the pins.

Pins may be straightened with an inexpensive pin-straightener purchased from most florists, or by using the empty hollow metal cartridge from an old ball-point pen as a lever to push them back in line.

It is also helpful to spray your container and pinholder with aerosol lysol (or spray paint) before you put them away. This not only retards subsequent bacterial development which will shorten plant life, but may save you a nasty infection if you are inadvertently cut by a pin.

5
Preserving and Treating Plant Material

Francisco José de Goya's artistic creed, "A composition is finished when its effect is true," may often be applied to the flower arrangements of today. In designing to obtain the desired effect, great latitude exists in the choice of materials for they may be fresh or dormant, dried or treated, and in any combination.

There are no limitations as to what can be preserved, dried, and treated, for each specimen will respond to many techniques. Thus the imaginative arranger can enjoy unlimited plant materials and can create them with but little effort and knowledge. Preserving garden and field flowers and foliage does, however, require planning ahead.

Air Drying

During the spring, summer, and fall you can find many kinds of straw flowers and everlastings which will dry naturally. Among the grasses, weeds, seed pods, and berries there are also thistles, milkweed pods, sumac seed heads, rose hips, cat-tails, pampas grass; lilac, wisteria, and hibiscus seed pods; tansy, Queen Anne's lace, and golden rod.

The smoke in "Aftermath of an Indian Raid" (plate 68) was created of two types of pampas grass; the bleached variety was purchased at the florist's, the air-dried variety was picked by the roadside. The strong lines of the arrows, which were clipped palmetto leaves, were wired at right angles to the charred driftwood. Two pinholders, one a cup-pinholder and one in the black ceramic vase, were used.

Flowers which dry readily include globe amaranth, lunaria (honesty), statice, baby's breath, lavender, Chinese lantern, liatris, globe thistle, and yarrow. Most of these flowers are easily cultivated. Strawflowers up to two inches in diameter come in white, shades of pink, bronze, lavender, and tones of yellow on plants which grow up to three feet tall. Dried strawflowers will retain their color for years.

The Chinese lanterns in plate 69 were arranged with a piece of wood painted black in a black ceramic container on a wooden slat base. Later they were allowed to air-dry in the arrangement simply by eliminating the water in the vase; there was little if any color change in them.

Such foliage plants as santolina and artemisia and many ornamental grasses all respond well.

Plant material to be dried should be cut as soon as the morning dew has evaporated and

94 Flowers and Foliage

68 AFTERMATH OF AN INDIAN RAID (Photo by Alwood Harvey)

Preserving and Treating Plant Material 95

69 CHINESE LANTERN (Photo by James Swan)

quite early in the morning. Best results are obtained when the blossoms have not quite attained their full bloom and are half to three-quarters open. The intense shades of primary colors are retained better than pastels.

Air-drying is a simple and very satisfactory technique. Usually it is best to bundle the stems of your plant material together and hang them upside down in a cool airy place. This also keeps the stems straight.

If you do not care about having straight stems, or if your material has a heavy straight stem naturally (such as cat-tails and pampas grass), just place it in a large container and let it dry by itself; but do not crowd your material so tightly that there is no air circulation around each specimen. It takes from ten days to two weeks for flowers to air-dry, depending upon atmospheric conditions.

All the flowers and grasses in the little composition in plate 70, arranged in a vitamin bottle sprayed beige and filled with styrofoam, were picked and air-dried by Nanette Gail Fields, who was thirteen at the time.

Some plant materials such as acorn caps and pinecones also dry naturally. In plate 71, Melinda Sue Fields cut the tips off some pinecones to create pinecone flowers which she used with acorn caps on a dry oak branch and a lovely ceramic figurine of a young girl day-dreaming. She was fifteen at the time she created this attractive composition, which has both textural and linear interest.

Tropical material, such as the coconut palm used in plate 72, also air-dries with no special treatment. "Holocaust" was an abstract arrangement created for a display at a New York State Judges' Council meeting. The strong vertical pipe, painted brown, with a dried twist of root balanced on it stabilizes the swirling inverted coconut palm on top and the spiraling flame-red anthurium and green yucca foliage at the base.

In the fall, pale green milkweed pods abound at the roadside. They also air-dry naturally with no special treatment. However, as they dry, they split open and liberate hundreds of airborne seeds. Therefore, it is advisable to slit each seed pod open carefully with a knife or thumb nail and remove the seeds before using the pods in arrangements.

In plate 73, an arrangement of all dry materials, milkweed pods and weathered wood are featured with two commercially dried tree cankers from Mexico on a burl base.

Silica Gel

There are commercial preparations such as silica gel (Flower Dri) which can be used to dry flowers. This is a chemical compound of harmless granular material which absorbs moisture rapidly. It is available from most florists and nurseries. When packed around the flowers, it removes the water in them without changing their color or form.

Large single blossoms hold their color and form best when cut at an advanced-bud to half-open stage; spike forms when the majority of the florets are fully opened. Tight buds of large flowers, such as roses, are too fleshy to process well, and full-blown open blossoms shatter too easily.

If your flowers wilt before they can be placed in the drying medium, revive them with water first and then pat them thoroughly dry with a towel.

Other Formulas

Flowers may be dried in sifted sea sand. This drying process takes about two weeks.

Flowers may also be dried in sifted borax. In this case, the flowers will dry in about three days to a week. Any longer time spent in the borax will cause discoloration.

Another formula which is quite successful as a drying agent is a mixture of equal parts of finely ground corn meal and powdered borax. To each quart of mix add three table spoons of un-iodized table salt. Do not use this mixture in a metal container.

Fine sand (builder's or beach varieties) may also be used as an extender to the silica gel or borax formulas; but this may slow the drying process slightly, for the sand is not absorbent.

The golden spider chrysanthemums in plate 74 were dried in an extended sand and silica gel mixture. They were combined with fresh yucca

SHIP AHOY (Photo by George E. Ernst)

VERNAL EQUINOX (Photo by James Swan)

WOOD AND ECHEVERIA
(Photo by George E. Ernst)

CIRCLES (Photo by George E. Ernst)

DAHLIAS, CERAMIC, AND METAL (Photo by George E. Ernst)

Preserving and Treating Plant Material 97

70 DRIED FLOWERS by Nanette Gail Fields
(Photo by Alwood Harvey)

71 **ACORN CAPS AND CONE FLOWERS** by
Melinda Sue Fields (Photo by James Swan)

Preserving and Treating Plant Material 99

72 HOLOCAUST (Photo by George E. Ernst)

100 Flowers and Foliage

73 MILKWEED PODS (Photo by George E. Ernst)

Preserving and Treating Plant Material   101

foliage and a dried maple whip in a cup-pinholder held by a home-made figure to create "Aspiration," a blue ribbon arrangement.

Drying Technique

Sift a layer of your chosen mixture about one inch deep into a box. A shoe box works well.

Place the spike form or foliage horizontally on this layer. Place the flower heads of round types of plant material upside down in this layer; leave the stems on the flowers in an erect position exposed to the air during the drying period, but strip the foliage from them.

Dry a few leaves separately if you want them.

Then sift your mixture over each flower until it is completely covered.

With multipetaled flowers, work some powder between the layers of petals before you place them in the box and then sift the powder gently over them.

Do not cover the box and do not crowd the specimens you are drying by placing too many in one box at the same time. The flowers should not touch each other during the drying process but should be completely surrounded by the mixture.

Store the box in a cool, well-ventilated place where it will not be disturbed. Drying time varies with the type of mixture you are using, the type of flower you are drying (delicate ones take less time than those with heavy-textured petals), and the atmospheric conditions (dampness and humidity will slow the drying process). Flowers are dry when they feel crisp to the touch.

At the end of the drying period, tip the container and carefully pour off the mixture to expose your flowers. When retrieving them, dust them gently with a clean artist's paint brush to remove any excess powder.

All of these formulas may be reused innumerable times. Sift them occasionally to remove any debris and store them in a covered container.

Storage and Use

Dried flowers may be stored in a covered box and are best when wrapped in tissue paper. A few moth balls and a little powdered borax will discourage household insects.

Store the box in a cool, well-ventilated place.

Dry flowers must be handled very carefully as they are very brittle. Dampness will cause them to become limp. For this reason, they are best used in arrangements in the fall after the heat has been turned on in your home.

Glycerine

Heavy-textured woody-stemmed foliage can last for years when conditioned in a solution of glycerine and water. (Glycerinized eucalyptus is frequently available from florists and nurseries in the fall.)

Use one part of glycerine and two parts of water. Make enough of this solution so that a

74 ASPIRATION (Photo by Bill Sevecke)

three-inch level can be maintained continuously in your container. Anti-freeze may be used in the same manner and proportions as glycerine.

75 PODOCARPUS AND COTTON FLOWERS
(Photo by **George E. Ernst**)

Cut an assortment of branches, deciduous or evergreen, some long, some short, some with straight lines and some which have interesting curves. Wash off any stains and discard damaged foliage. Split or mash the stem ends up to approximately two inches (this aids in the absorption of the solution) and remove any foliage which will be under water in the solution. It takes from two to three weeks for the branches to be completely conditioned. Recut the stem ends about once a week, and remove about an inch at each cutting, for this keeps the capillaries free and unclogged, thus aiding your plant material to absorb the glycerine and water solution.

If you have a good evergreen branch that you wish to save, by all means condition it with the solution while it is in place in your arrangement, although getting the proper depth of liquid in a vase may take more solution than you would have to use in a conditioning jar.

The podocarpus in plate 75 was glycerinized in the bronze usubata which held the arrangement. The sanshuike (three-material) Shoka consisted of dried cotton flowers (dyed red) and date palm.

Plant material conditioned with glycerine and water will remain flexible and pliable permanently, and treated evergreens do not have needle drop. Conditioned material can, therefore, be utilized in much the same manner as fresh plant material, although there is a color change toward brown hues in material that has been conditioned.

Glycerinized material can be used in an arrangement without water if the other plant material does not require it. It can also be combined with fresh material and placed in a container to which water is added.

In plate 76, water kept the bright red anemone and the azalea fresh, although the magnolia foliage and the ti leaf were glycerinized. (Anemones, incidentally, respond extremely well to the silica gel technique for drying.) The container is a black ceramic import.

In plate 77, two pieces of natural elongated sponge, two air-dried pink-beige hydrangeas, two pieces of glycerinized iris foliage, and two glycerinized hosta leaves were used to create an "Experiment in Brown" in a brown and tan thumbprint vase by Estelle Halper on a natural brown cedar shingle base. The glycerinized foliage retained its surface texture completely but the treatment changed its color from green to brown.

76 MAGNOLIA, ANEMONE, AND AZALEA
(Photo by James Swan)

77 **EXPERIMENT IN BROWN** (Photo by James Swan)

Preserving and Treating Plant Material

Long-lasting Greens

An Illinois florist, Harold C. Cook, recently developed a preservative formula which lengthens the life of evergreens without changing their color, texture or quality. Make a fresh cut and then mash the fibers of the ends of your branches and place them in a large bucket or container. Combine one gallon of boiling water with four teaspoons of Clorox or any chlorinated household bleach, two cups of light Karo, or other syrup, and four tablespoons of Green Gard Micronized Iron; pour several inches of this solution into your container and allow the evergreens to remain in it overnight or longer. Branches may be left in the preservative for several days if desired.

The combination of crushed fibers and hot preservative increases capillary action and helps the branches to absorb the preservative. Evergreen branches treated in this mixture will last several weeks longer and appear fresher than untreated ones. It may be used with equal success on both broadleaf and needled evergreens.

The blue-green Pfitzer branches in plate 78 were treated with the preservative for two days and then combined with a red candle and some weathered wood to create a simple, gay, and long-lasting holiday decoration. Care should always be taken when using candles to replace them with taller ones whenever necessary, so that the flame will not be in proximity to the plant material.

Skeletonizing Leaves

At any time of the year, but particularly in the fall when leaf texture is declining, leaves may be skeletonized. Stripping the thin layer of "skin" down to the skeleton is a relatively simple but slow process.

An old hair brush or shoe brush is the most important tool, and the bristles should be firm but not too stiff. A square of carpeting tacked to a piece of plywood is also required.

Place the leaf on the carpeting, top side up, and hold it gently but firmly as you tap it lightly with the brush. Gentle but repeated tapping is the key to cleaning the leaf. Reverse it often and tap the under side as well, checking it frequently by holding it up to the light. This treatment will remove the leaf's outer skin, and all that remains will be the fine veins.

Leaf skeletons may be preserved and given better body by spraying them with an aerosol clear shellac after they have been stripped.

78 PFITZER JUNIPER, CANDLE, AND WOOD
(Photo by James Swan)

Oak, maple, magnolia, or any firm, well-textured leaf will prove suitable for this treatment and will add an interesting accent to an arrangement.

Four skeletonized leaves, an air-dried artichoke, a pine cone, and some plastic rods and plastic tubing were used in plate 79 to create an airy free-style composition in a cup-pinholder on a black wooden base to illustrate the use of dry material in "Textures and Tones."

79 TEXTURES AND TONES (Photo by James Swan)

6
Driftwood and Weathered Wood

The many and varied forms of wood, branches, and roots which may be found have exciting possibilities for the arranger who enjoys utilizing nature's treasures. Some are actually completed sculptures in themselves and merely need mounting to set them off properly, while others can be carved, sawed, nailed, glued, and combined with other pieces to create exciting containers, accessories or structures.

A budded branch and some pachysandra in a cup-pinholder (plate 80) which was exhibited at the Westchester Art Workshop, or some native bamboo and some hen-and-chickens (plate 81) are two of the many materials which can be used in this naturalistic composition. The basic structure was made from a piece of driftwood nailed to a slice of wood. This long-lasting arrangement needs only the addition of water to the cup-pinholder to keep it fresh and springlike.

Technically, driftwood is wood which has been immersed in water, and that which has been in salt water often turns a whitish hue. Weathered wood is wood which has been aged in the woods or field and usually remains a warmer brown color.

Sand, wind, rain, snow, insects, in fact all phases of nature aid in forming and giving surface texture and tone to the various trees which have provided these pieces of driftwood and weathered wood.

The three pieces of date palm in plate 82 may technically be considered "wood." They were bent into the desired curves after they had been immersed in hot water long enough to soften them; then they were anchored in a cup-pinholder to frame and accentuate the swirling lines of the sculptured girl by Rima.

Usually weathered wood requires extensive cleaning to remove excess soil and rot, but care should be taken to salvage an interesting natural patina or weathering if it exists. An old tooth brush, potato brush, scrubbing brush, or even a steel lint-remover brush may be helpful to clean out grooves and crevices. All rotten and pulpy sections should be scraped out with a knife. It is also a good idea to use an aerosol insect spray on weathered wood when cleaning it. Automobile body shops and many furniture refinishing shops have facilities for sandblasting your wood if you wish to create a smooth highly-sanded surface.

Wood may be used in any position in a creative composition, but often mounting it on a wooden or metal dowel will enhance its inherent qualities and set it off to best advantage. When elevating it,

80 **BIRD AND PACHYSANDRA** (Photo by Alwood Harvey)

81 BIRD AND BAMBOO (Photo by Alwood Harvey)

82 DATE PALM AND GIRL (Photo by George E. Ernst)

Driftwood and Weathered Wood 111

83 SHIP AHOY (Photo by George E. Ernst)

Flowers and Foliage

bronze Edward Schillaci figures. Two tall stalks of gladiolus in a cup-pinholder, partially diffused by the dried pieces of fungus, complete the blue ribbon arrangement called "Vernal Equinox," which was created for a flower show school.

"Indian War Dance" (plate 85) was created by pruning an interesting weathered branch and adding a dried artichoke head. The dry artichoke was preferable to a fresh one because of its lighter weight as well as its brown hue.

84 **VERNAL EQUINOX (Photo by James Swan)**

however, compensating weight must be found for the base to prevent physical instability.

In "Ship Ahoy" (plate 83), two pieces of driftwood were firmly impaled on metal dowels. Cup-pinholders were balanced on top and on the wood to hold the pink gladioli and gladiolus foliage.

An unusual five-foot piece of broken and weathered bamboo was nailed to a burl base in plate 84. It formed an airy note with the attenuated

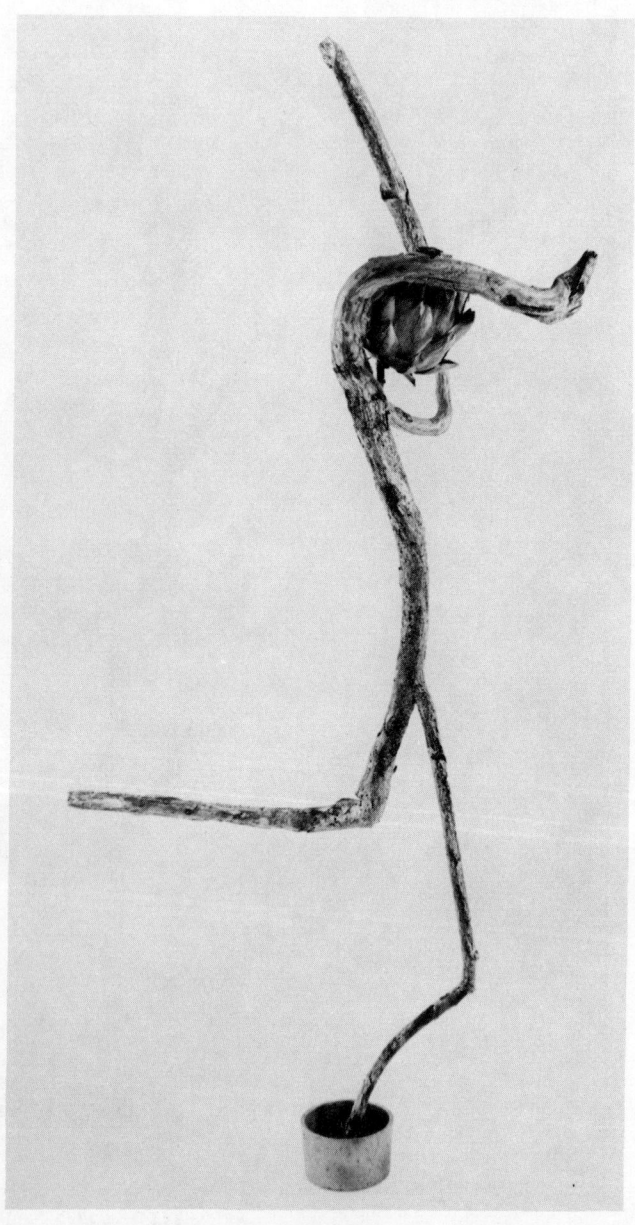

85 **INDIAN WAR DANCE (Photo by James Swan)**

86 CAPRICORN (Photo by James Swan)

Plate 86, "Capricorn," features a whittled and stained piece of wood with two sansevieria "ears" stapled to the top. Grapes and grape ivy were used at the base, covering the cup-pinholder.

Liquid wax, linseed oil, wood stains, and varnish will all bring out the wood grain and darken the wood. Often this will also cause the surface grain to be raised, making it necessary to resand the wood between applications.

Wood may be bleached by using equal parts of water and household bleach; the longer you soak the wood and the stronger the bleach in proportion to the solution, the whiter the wood will become. Because of fumes, do this chore out-of-doors whenever possible.

Wood may also be bleached by throwing it into a swimming pool for the summer (if you have one, and if your family does not object) and permitting the chlorine to act upon it.

In plate 87, nine different pieces of driftwood were glued and nailed together to create a four-foot abstract sculpture. Some of the pieces required bleaching to help them match the tonal qualities of the other pieces used. Three blue-gray echeverias, *Gibbiflora metallica,* were the plant material added as a fresh accent to the composition.

A neolithic bluish undersea effect can be created on the wood surface by painting it with a mixture of one quarter of a cup of clear household ammonia, one teaspoon of copper sulphate (available in most hobby shops or drug stores), and one teaspoon of Elmer's glue. For a deeper tone, repaint the surface several times. An uneven effect is usually most desirable. Incidentally, although porous surfaces respond best to this surface treatment, cup-pinholders and accessories have been successfully matched to the treated wood by using the same formula but doubling the glue proportion.

In plate 88, the weathered wood, the inverted branch, and the cup-pinholder were all treated with this copper sulphate formula. Pink tulips were used to complete the line-mass composition.

Wood may be painted and repainted to any color with a wide variety of aerosol spray paints, and some interesting metallic tones may be found in automobile spray paints. Whether you color the wood a solid tone or let some of the natural color and grain show through is entirely a matter of personal preference.

The "All Foliage" blue ribbon arrangement in plate 89 utilizes both weathered wood and a base of plywood which my daughters fished out of the Hudson River. A little sanding and some acrylic paint made the tones compatible.

The foliage consists of bronze rex begonia leaves, dark green variegated sansevieria, and pale gray-green succulents, all from houseplants. The two cup-pinholders were painted to match the wood, so that in the actual arrangement they were barely visible; in the photograph, however, you can see them quite clearly—a perfect example of how color often diffuses form.

Plate 90 is another blue ribbon arrangement entitled "A Walk in the Woods." An assortment of vines, branches, and weathered wood were nailed and glued together, then combined with three pieces of dried fungus, some skunk cabbage, and two forced branches from a horse chestnut, set in a cup-pinholder on a burl base.

Exotic red torch ginger, self-foliage, and two pieces of gray driftwood were used with a freeform blue-gray ceramic to form the composition in plate 91.

Driftwood and Weathered Wood

87 WOOD AND ECHEVERIA (Photo by George E. Ernst)

116 *Flowers and Foliage*

88 WOOD AND TULIPS (Photo by George E. Ernst)

Driftwood and Weathered Wood 117

89 ALL FOLIAGE (Photo by Bill Sevecke)

Flowers and Foliage

90 A WALK IN THE WOODS (Photo by Bill Sevecke)

Driftwood and Weathered Wood 119

91 TORCH GINGER AND WOOD (Photo by James Swan)

7
Containers

The roots of many of our concepts in flower arranging come from Japan, where flower arranging has been an art for more than fifteen hundred years. According to Mr. Senei Ikenobo, the forty-fifth headmaster of the Ikenobo School, the container sets the tenor for a flower arrangement; for example, as in a usubata—which creates the appearance of a quiet reflecting pool, or as in a suiban—which has a horizontal quality akin to an informal landscape or in an arrangement such as a Futakabu Shoka or Moribana, or as in a bronze moon. (See plates 92 and 93.)

In Western arranging, our contemporary design also considers this a very basic concept, for to ignore the lower third or more of your composition would be totally impossible.

Containers may be anything from a cup-pinholder to a ceramic vase or copper pipe, anything which can hold or support the plant material. If fresh-cut plant material is used, needless to say, it is vital to provide adequate water. Our medium is at best very short-lived and it would be the epitome of foolhardiness not to make provision for its preservation.

If you have made a good construction or container, it is often interesting and challenging to use it in different ways. Plates 94 and 95 both feature my four-foot strap metal hand-made space-enclosing form which supports its own cup-pinholder.

The arrangement which uses heliconia and yucca in plate 94 was an experiment in modern design for a New York State Judges' Council meeting.

The arrangement which features *Allium gigantium* in plate 95 was used to denote "Tivoli" at an international party at the Rockefeller Pocantico Hills Estate. The alliums, which ranged in shades from pale pink to deep purple, suggested the balloons and gaiety of this well-known amusement park and the sweeping side of the strap metal suggests the roller coaster.

Metal hoops are often found in hardware stores and plumbing supply shops; metal loops of strap metal or lightweight tubing are easy to bend and shape and can be glued with epoxy, soldered or welded.

"Circles" (plate 96), created for this chapter, was made of bent strap metal. Two strips of palm were curled and stapled to repeat the circular forms of the metal, and two dahlias were added in a cup-pinholder for a fresh accent.

It is interesting to compare the flower arrangements made by potters when they wish to display something in their own containers. The flowers are often relegated to a secondary position and

Containers

121

92 CLASSICAL BRONZE CONTAINERS (Photo by Richard Hong)

93 CONTEMPORARY CERAMIC CONTAINERS (Photo by Richard Hong)

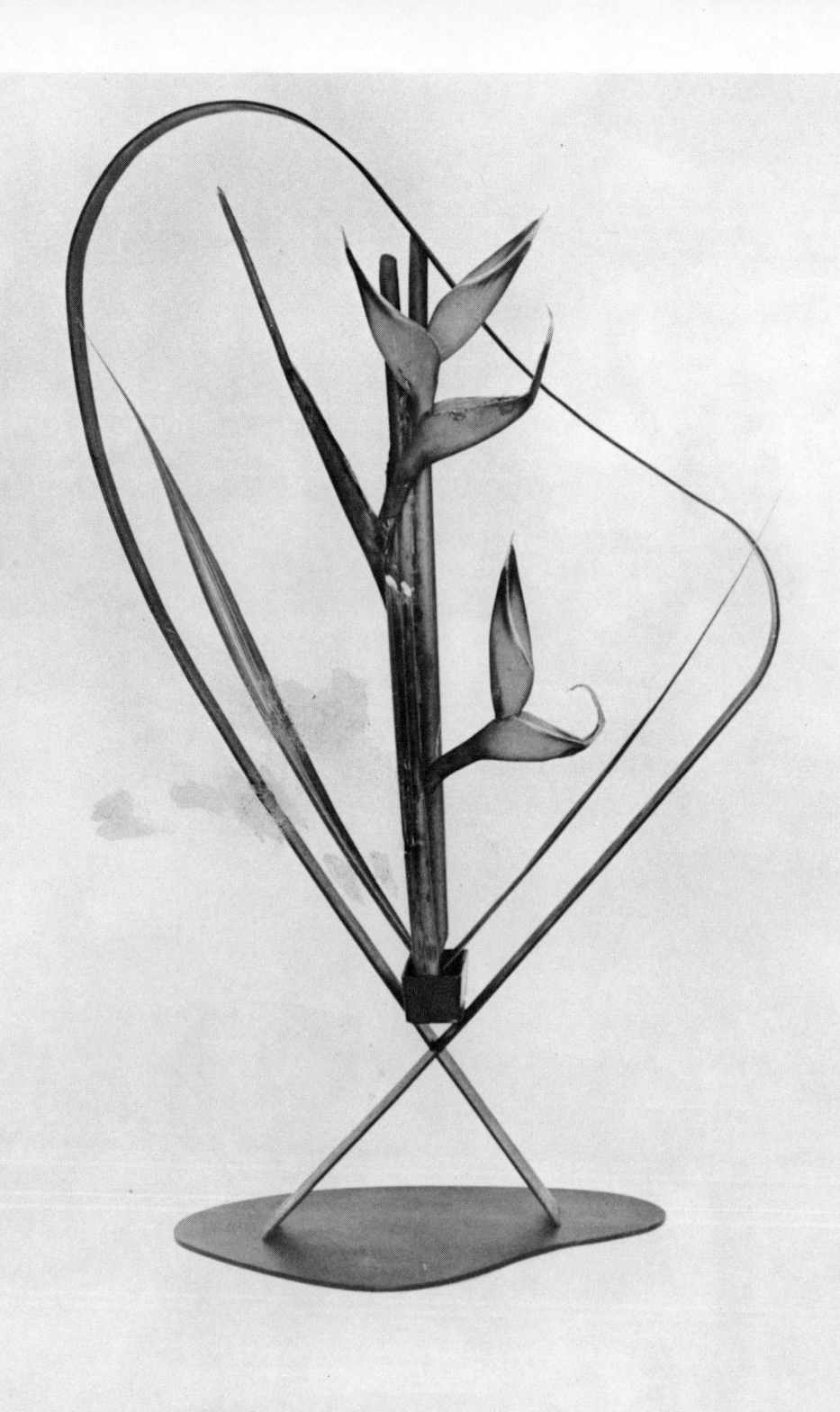

94 HELICONIA (Photo by Alwood Harvey)

95 **TIVOLI** (Photo by Alwood Harvey)

124

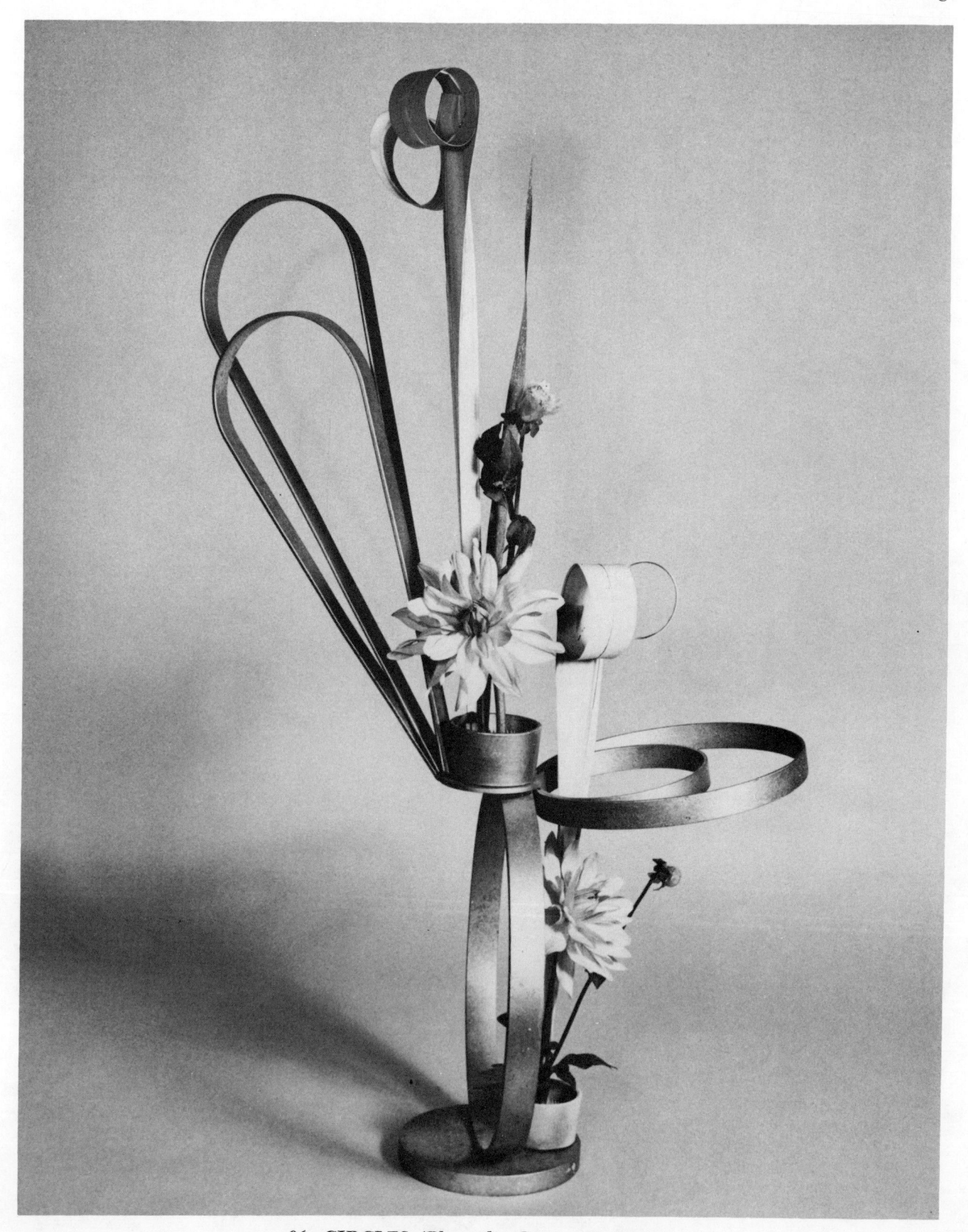

Flowers and Foliage

96 CIRCLES (Photo by George E. Ernst)

Containers

97 **CZECHOSLOVAKIA** (Photo by Bill Sevecke)

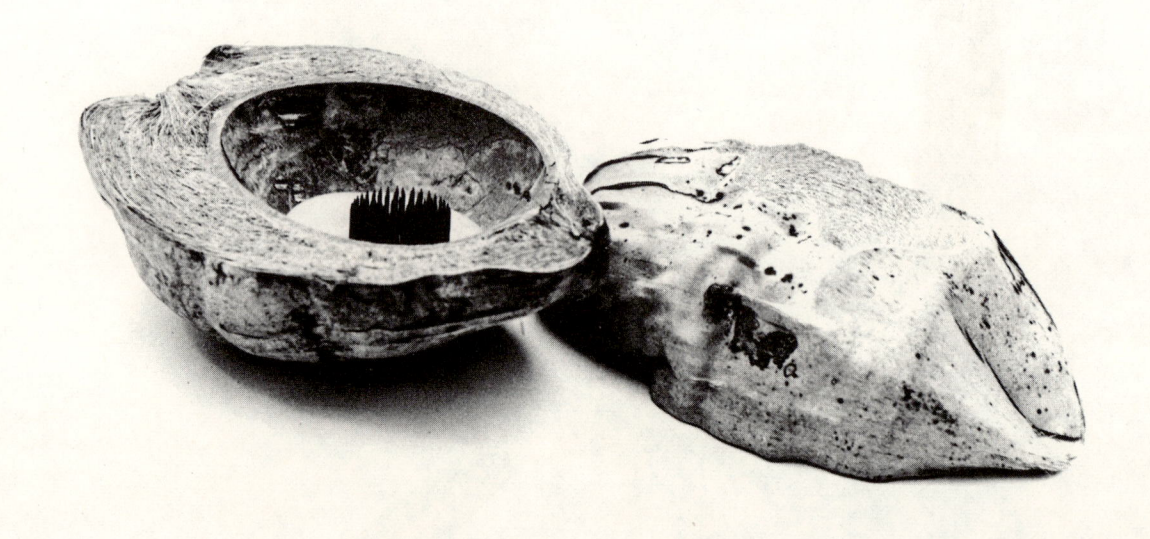

98 COCONUT HULL CONTAINERS (Photo by Richard Hong)

just peep over the lip of the vase; they certainly do not compete in interest with the container itself.

At one time, arrangements were required to be one and one-half times the greatest height or length of the container used; this is no longer considered a truism.

Arrangements may be any size, although a rectangular form, whether horizontal or vertical, is always more interesting than a square one. The only prerequisite is that the overall composition should fit and suit the space in which it is to be placed, whether in a show or at home.

Containers may be of any size or dimension and, in fact, their very size may determine the kind of composition created. A large container would require a huge composition or material that compensates in visual weight for the size of the container. An upright vase needs material which extends downward from its lip to minimize the size.

Although a number of my friends are potters, and I am fortunate in that I can obtain attractive pots from them, I have often found that it is necessary to make some changes in their containers; *e.g.,* drilling additional holes in the sides of a container above the water line (with an electric drill and the carborundum bit used by a bathroom tile man), through which material may be inserted diagonally or horizontally as a design concept develops. And my friends will say: "But

Containers

why didn't you tell me you wanted a hole there when I was making that piece?"

A multimouthed container, or one with several holes in it, may have some areas left open and unused to provide spatial relief and interest, as in plate 28. Multiple dominances in a design might require a container with multiple mouths, or the use of several containers or cup-pinholders.

Two "centers of interest," the two yellow football chrysanthemums used in the two cup-pinholders in plate 97, represented the roofs of the golden minarets of Prague, Czechoslovakia, at an international party where the floral decorations interpreted various countries. A metal rod, washer, and screw supported the upper cup-pinholder. Three Royal-poinciana pods were softened in hot water and then bent into the desired curves to suggest the outdoor stone staircases of that city, and the horse chestnut foliage represented one of the trees popular there.

Many of nature's discards make excellent containers for perceptive arrangers. A walnut shell might be excellent for a miniature arrangement; and a coconut hull (plate 98) is a good medium-sized container.

Many of nature's treasures form containers which are both interesting and challenging. Some may need to be mounted on a base with a wooden dowel or threaded pipe and a washer and bolt. Some may not hold water; thus a cup-pinholder (or tuna fish can and plain pinholder) may have to be included.

A friend once brought me the handsome antler used in plate 99. Its excellent design possibilities were best utilized when it was mounted on a rod that could also support a cup-pinholder. *Cedrus glauca atlantica* and yellow sunlit gladioli were added to interpret "Vacation Memories," which won a blue ribbon.

There are many man-made materials which are relatively easy to shape into suitable and imaginative containers. Flexible metal such as plumber's lead, pewter, brass and copper tubing (as in plate 100) or metal screening (as in plate 101) and aluminum wire can all be cut, bent, and manipulated readily even without specialized equipment.

The homemade nishuike-type tubular container used in plate 102 with Scotch broom and crocus was flat screening soldered together with a front hole cut into it. The plant material was inserted into a cup-pinholder at the bottom.

99 VACATION MEMORIES (Photo by Alwood Harvey)

Some metals can be reworked only if they have been heated or annealed, and these would not be suitable media for those without the necessary special equipment. Automobile body repair shops, however, are equipped to do simple spot welding if you bring your materials and requirements to them.

Sometimes a container may be no more complex than a single cup-pinholder and a base, as in plate 103. This is particularly suitable when you

100 COPPER TUBING CONTAINER (Photo by Richard Hong)

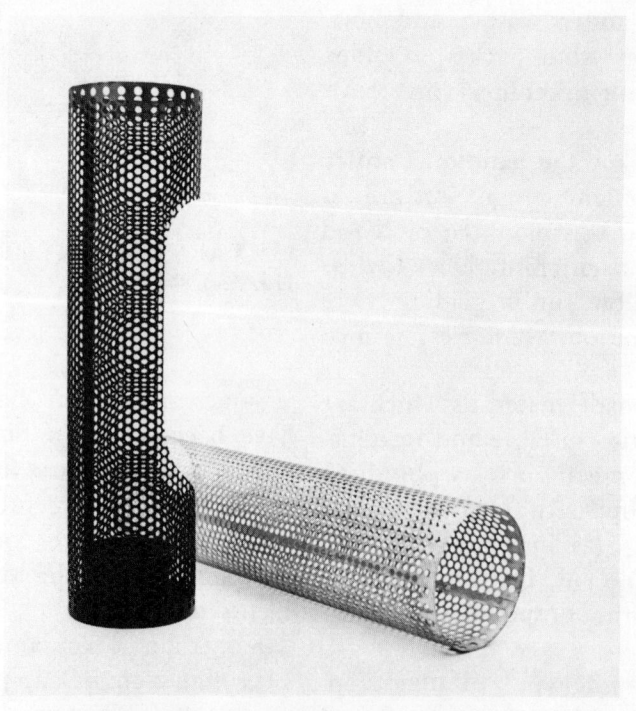

101 NISHUIKE SCREEN CONTAINER (Photo by Richard Hong)

102 BROOM AND CROCUS (Photo by James Swan)

103 **BOUILLABAISSE** (Photo by James Swan)

Containers

are working with a figurine (and do not need the added distraction of a ceramic container.) In "Bouillabaisse," gladioli and gladiolus foliage were combined with barnacle-encrusted floats threaded through two Virginia creeper vines in a cup-pinholder partially hidden by two martynia pods. The little fisherman by Ginnie Gilson completes this composition on a cryptomeria base.

Wood may also be cut to form interesting containers such as those shown in plate 104; the basic pattern and grain of the wood greatly enhance each construction (or may be completely obliterated by paint, if so desired).

The hexagonal container was used in plate 105 with glycerinized eucalyptus, dry pods, Scotch broom, and clipped palm in a pinholder. (If the materials required water, a cup-pinholder or liner of glass, metal, or plastic would, of course, be necessary.)

Lava rock and osmunda fiber both make provocative containers, as in plate 106. A hole in the center for the cup-pinholder may be readily shaped or enlarged with a penknife.

Plastic tubing, rods, and plastic filaments are available in many lumber yards and hobby shops. They too have possibilities for creative containers. Some types of plastic sheets which may be sawed and glued can also be shaped with heat from a home oven.

In plate 107, "Ecology," three rods of clear plastic with imprisoned bubbles were used in place of a conventional container. A piece of weathered wood was balanced on top of one to create a strong horizontal line. A cup-pinholder which held red geraniums and geranium foliage was balanced on another to add the vertical thrust. The third was polished with jeweler's rouge and left uncovered.

Self-hardening clays and those which may be fired in a home oven are also available and can be shaped through slab or coil techniques or can be molded and hollowed in your hands. Interesting freeform shapes may be obtained by any of these methods, and surfaces can be incised, painted, or glazed to create excellent textures and patterns.

Glass has many possibilities, too. Sheet glass can be cut at home with a special diamond-edge tool or you can utilize the skills of your local glazier. In any case, be sure to file or grind the edges to a safe, smooth finish. Sheet glass is available in clear, white, smoke, or black varieties, or can be special-ordered in colors.

104 **WOOD CONTAINERS (Photo by Richard Hong)**

Opaque sheet glass can also be used for handsome bases and is every bit comparable to lacquer, but considerably less expensive.

Glass slag, too, is often available, and one of the best sources for it, other than a glass foundry, is at your local pet shop where chunks of slag (as well as many other interesting rocks) are sold by the pound for use in aquarium landscaping and decoration.

Glass tubes in a variety of sizes can be purchased at the drug store or hobby shop, and when mounted in a suitable stand can become effective receptacles or accessories. With a small blow torch you can shape glass tubes into many interesting forms. A construction of glass can be glued together with plastic cement such as epoxy.

Various materials, identical in form or not, may

105 EUCALYPTUS RIKKA (Photo by James Swan)

106 LAVA AND OSMUNDA CONTAINERS
(Photo by Richard Hong)

107 ECOLOGY (Photo by George E. Ernst)

108 **YARROW AND CALATHEAS** (Photo by James Swan)

Containers

109 TIN CAN CONTAINERS (Photo by George E. Ernst)

be stacked upon each other to create a container. For example, a small salad bowl may be glued to an inverted glass ash tray to create a footed compote. Identical compotes may be tiered, or stacked right-side up, or inverted. Glass or plastic may be combined with opaque materials, such as wood or ceramics, to create a floating effect. Surface embellishments can be added or omitted. The possibilities are unlimited.

The container in plate 108 is a tall olive jar, painted, rolled in sand, and then repainted to create an interesting texture. The wet paint acts as a glue and holds the surface sand. The base is a wood burl. A twisted root, which has a rather surrealistic feeling, was washed and peeled to form the line material. The arrangement was done to illustrate this chapter. Two yellow yarrows and three calatheas are the plant material in this all-dry composition.

Tin cans can also be used for similar containers, and they may be stacked, with the bottoms glued together, for greater height, as in plate 109. They may be decorated with paint; the tops of the cans shown were further embellished with sand, toothpicks, and rope.

Aluminum cans or galvanized steel cans are better than tin because they do not rust. Cans, of course, are lighter in weight than jars and considerably less breakable.

Artificial fruits and vegetables, such as the cantaloupe and the corn shown in plate 110, also make excellent containers. An opening suitable for the pinholder can easily be cut with a keyhole saw. Since these containers are not particularly flat on the bottom, it is a good idea to stabilize the pinholder (and thus the plant material) with styrofoam-type sticky-clay.

A Swiss cheese philodendron leaf and two Egyptian tree onion stalks were used in a cut artificial cantaloupe in plate 111. The base is a wooden shingle. The arrangement could be titled "Open House."

By the way, the use of fresh-cut fruits and vegetables is rarely advisable as a container, partly because of spoilage and partly because of its attraction for fruit flies, *et cetera*. While it might be suitable for an occasion of short duration at home, it would not be acceptable for a flower show.

Styrofoam is another exciting medium with which to work, for it is easily molded and shaped, can be cut with a knife or saw, can be glued, and

110 CANTALOUPE AND CORN CONTAINERS (Photo by Richard Hong)

111 **OPEN HOUSE** (Photo by James Swan)

Containers 137

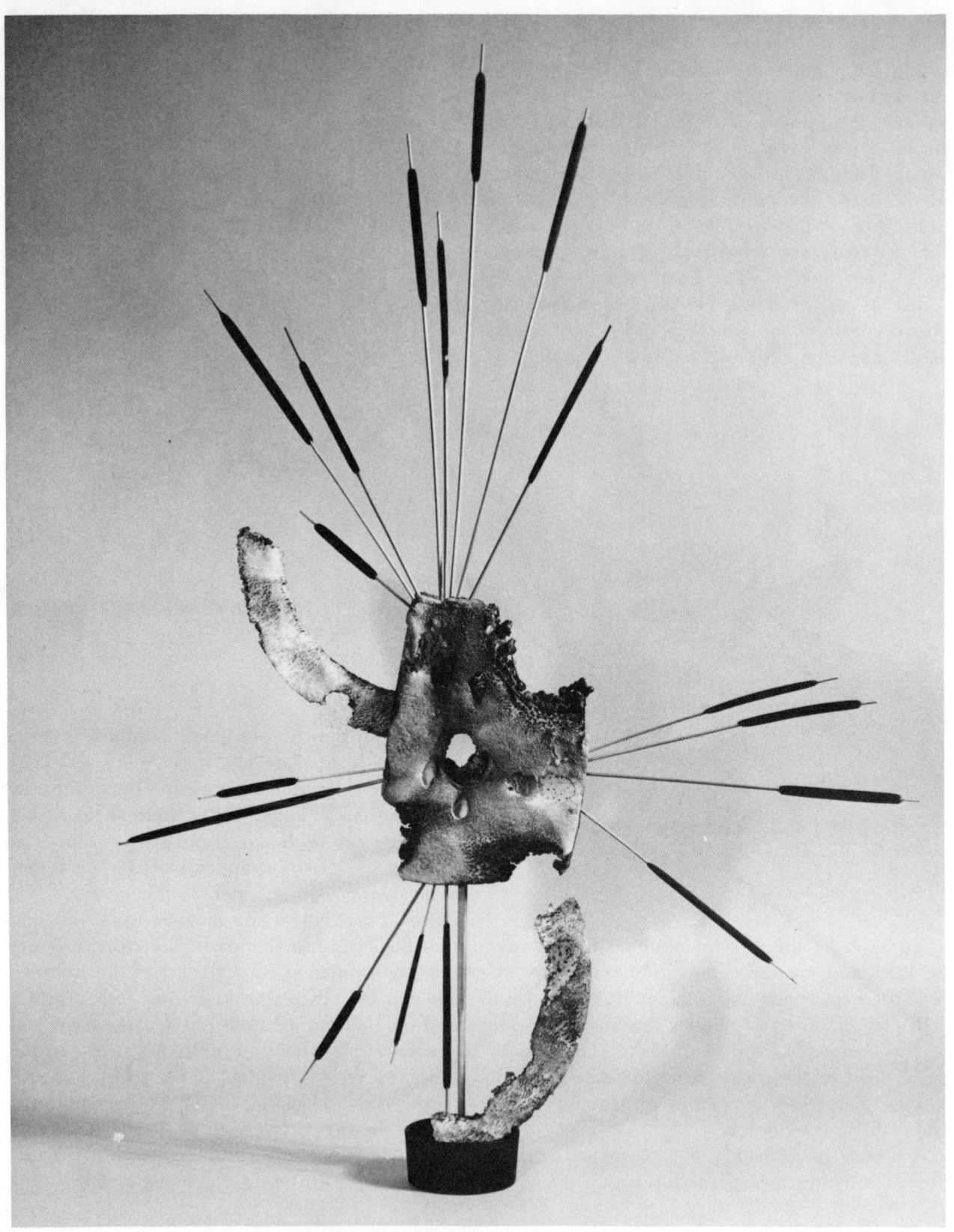

112 **APOLLO—THE AGE OF AQUARIUS** (Photo by George E. Ernst)

can also be sprayed or painted. If the paint used is not specially designed for styrofoam, an interesting Swiss cheese effect may be obtained, for the application of paint will cause the styrofoam to melt. It also melts from the application of heat in as low an intensity as that obtained from a candle flame. (This should be an outdoor project as the fumes are rather noxious.)

In plate 112, "Apollo—the Age of Aquarius," the styrofoam was modeled, cut, glued, sprayed, burnt, and painted. The small cat-tails were inserted in it to create a radiating effect, and the entire construction, which is quite lightweight, was balanced on a bamboo rod in a cup-pinholder.

113 BASKET AND CERAMIC CONTAINERS (Photo by Richard Hong)

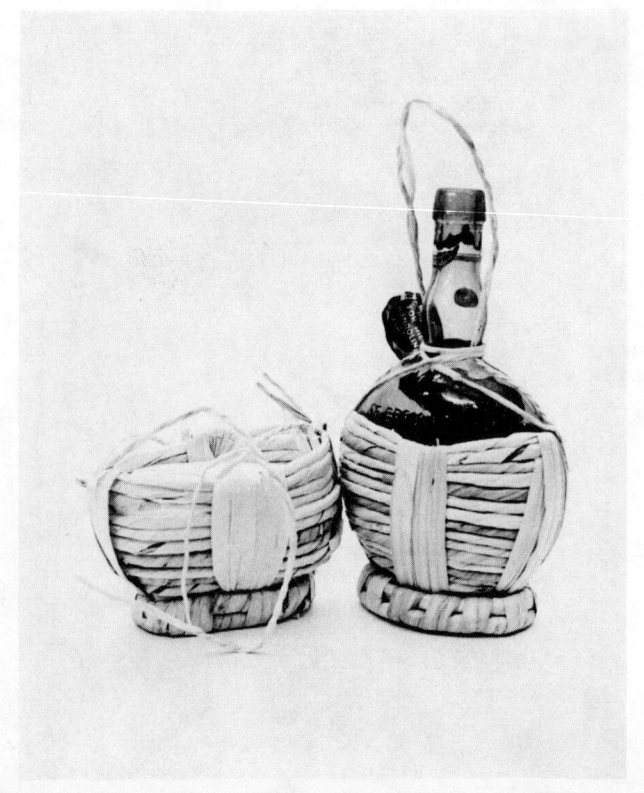

114 CHIANTI BOTTLE CONTAINER (Photo by Richard Hong)

There is no limit to the materials which may be used and combined to create containers except, perhaps, one's imagination. Price or basic cost, too, in no way indicates the intrinsic value of the completed creation. After all, art should be pursued in the nature and spirit of adventure to avoid being handicapped by preconceived ideas about utility and beauty.

A prosaic bread basket with a cup-holder or a broken container which has interesting shapes or angles may present intriguing possibilities for a container, as in plate 113.

It is even possible, as in plate 114, to separate the glass from a Chianti bottle and use the basket as a container—with styrofoam for a dry-material arrangement, or foil-wrapped oasis for plant materials which require water.

Just as the camera is a medium quite different from the brush, so the art of the creative flower arranger is different from the art of the painter—although as a flower arranger you may utilize a brush and paints, a hammer and nails, a saw and blowtorch. Skill develops with practice, and necessity or creativity often leads to imaginative solutions for the placement of flowers and plant material in any composition or design. Art, to be truly art and not just a craft, must be true to its own medium, mastering every phase of it.

8
Basic Mechanics

What you need for flower arranging is determined by the type of arrangement you are planning to make. If you are working with heavy branches or driftwood, a saw, nails, and appropriate equipment would be needed. If you are shaping leaves, sharp scissors would be a necessity.

Any type of equipment that does the job for you is suitable: wire, tape or clay, all will hold things in place. But regardless of what you use, you must adapt to two limitations:

1. Whatever you use should help to preserve your plant material in good condition for the length of its natural life cycle.

2. Whatever you use should not be openly visible in the finished composition. Mechanics are like basic cosmetics and undergarments—they may pull, push, twist, shape, pad, bind, but should not show, or, if they do, they should enhance the composition.

Basic equipment usually involves the items shown in plate 115: a good sharp pair of spring-pruning shears for cutting heavier branches, a pair of snips or scissors for lighter weight cutting, some thin and medium gauge wire, pinholders and cup-pinholders, sticky clay (which now comes in a roll instead of a solid package—the varieties marked "for styrofoam" are strongest and best), floral tape (both green and brown, although it is also available in other colors), and spray paint to change the color of your pinholders.

A good pinholder is essential; the heavier it is and the closer the pins, the better the pinholder. Those made of plastic are not good because they do not add enough weight and stability to hold the flowers.

A cup-pinholder (they come in round, oval, crescent, and square shapes) is also useful; but an arranger can economize and make one with a tunafish can sprayed black or brown and a pinholder clayed into it. The pinholder or needle-point holder holds the plant material in the design position desired, according to how it is impaled, whether the desired position is vertical, diagonal, or horizontal.

Plant material impaled on a pinholder will not be harmed in any way. Capillary action brings the water up the stem to the flowers as long as a clean cut has been made. The pinholder should always be sterile and clean.

It is a good idea to spray the pins and, in fact, the entire pinholder a color compatible with the container in order to make it diffuse more readily into the design, thus requiring less material to cover it up. Metallic brass pins should always be sprayed because they are particularly easy to see.

Waterlogged oasis is often used by commercial

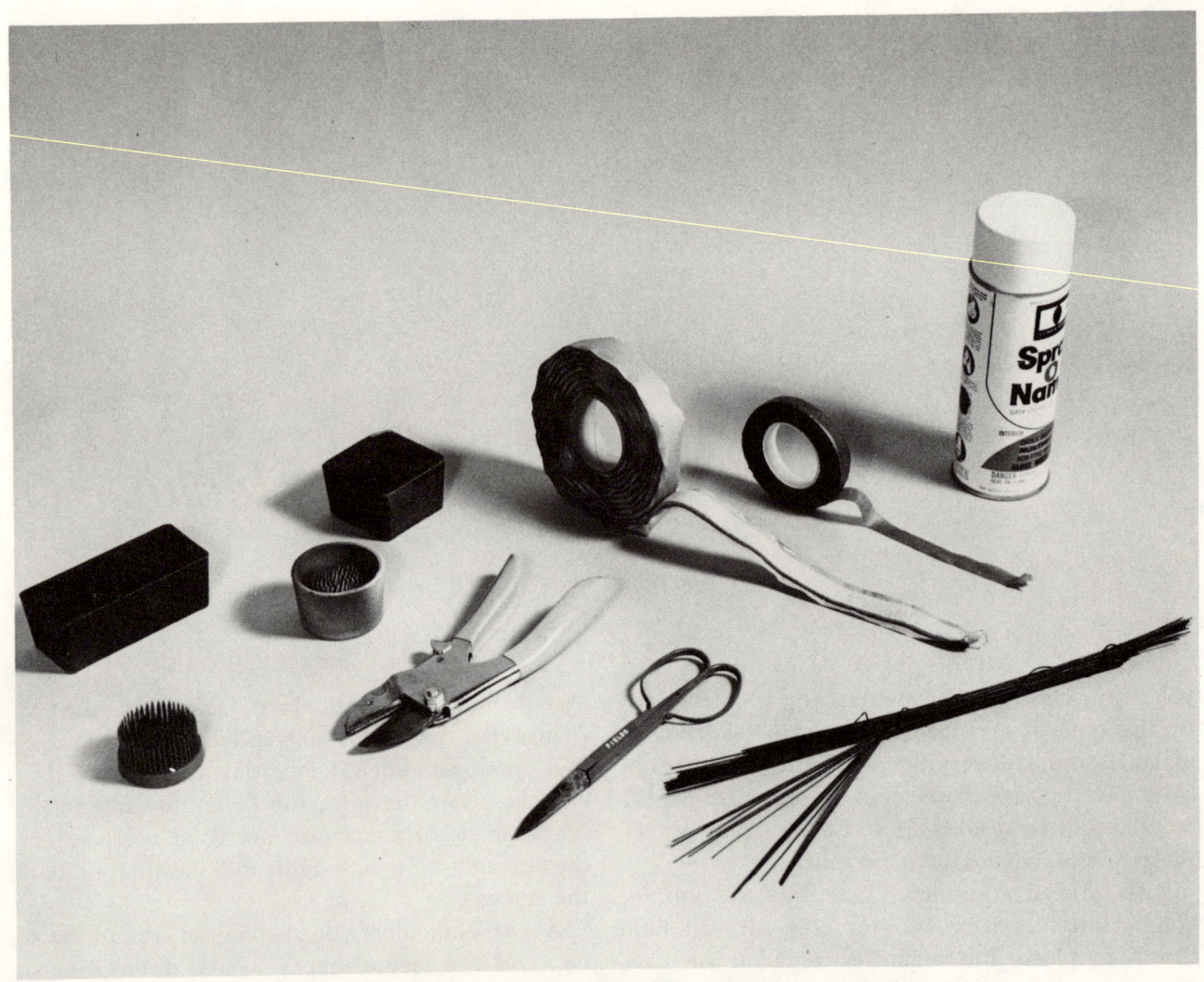

115 TOOLS OF THE TRADE (Photo by George E. Ernst)

florists in creating their designs, primarily because it is cheaper. This is false economy for the flower arranger, however, because it is not reusable, as is a pinholder. Once holes have been made in it by the impaled plant material, they are there permanently. Oasis is also lightweight and thus does not add physical stability or bottom weight to your design. In addition to this, oasis tends to clog the capillaries in the stems of the plant material.

If you are working in a deep vase, it is often helpful to fill it half way up with sand or bird gravel, then add a little melted wax on top and imbed your pinholder in it. With this type of permanent mechanics, you can add weight and stability to your container and also find it easier to anchor your plant material. Be sure, however, to allow for enough depth—at least a half-inch of water over the top of the pins and at least a half-inch between the water level and the lip of the container to prevent spills.

Knowledge of the Japanese technique of splints and kubari (forked branches) is also helpful if you are working with heavy branches. This Nageire technique would take the place of the permanent mechanics mentioned above or may be used in conjunction with it. A forked branch is wired or fitted at a right angle to the branch being inserted; it acts to counterbalance the cantilevered weight. If the entire joint is under the water level

Basic Mechanics

of the container, the branch will, of course, receive an adequate supply of water and remain fresh. Two branches, one of pine and one of semi-dormant lilac, are shown in the rectangular cup-pinholder in plate 116.

Plant material may be inserted in a pinholder in any position. The basic weight of the pinholder helps to balance the weight placed in it.

Just because plant material is straight does not mean that it must stay that way. In plate 116, a fresh cat-tail was bent into a curved form before the stem dried, then placed in the round cup-pinholder next to a straight one. It had been placed between the webs of a terrace chair for a few days to establish the curve.

A fresh, green branch may also be shaped into an interesting curve simply by bending it gently with a slight twisting motion. The one in the square cup-pinholder in plate 116 was bent into a curve and a reverse curve form.

Dry material may also be shaped with the same twisting motion after it has been soaked in warm water; thorough immersion makes gentle manipulation possible.

The Ikenobo School of Ikebana has recently come out with a pinholder on an extension suction base which can be fitted into a tall vase to provide the basic mechanics of an elevated pinholder, or a substitute for the kubari. It is shown in plate 117.

116 **BENDING BRANCHES** (Photo by George E. Ernst)

117 PINHOLDERS (Photo by Richard Hong)

118 HOSE CLAMP (Photo by Richard Hong)

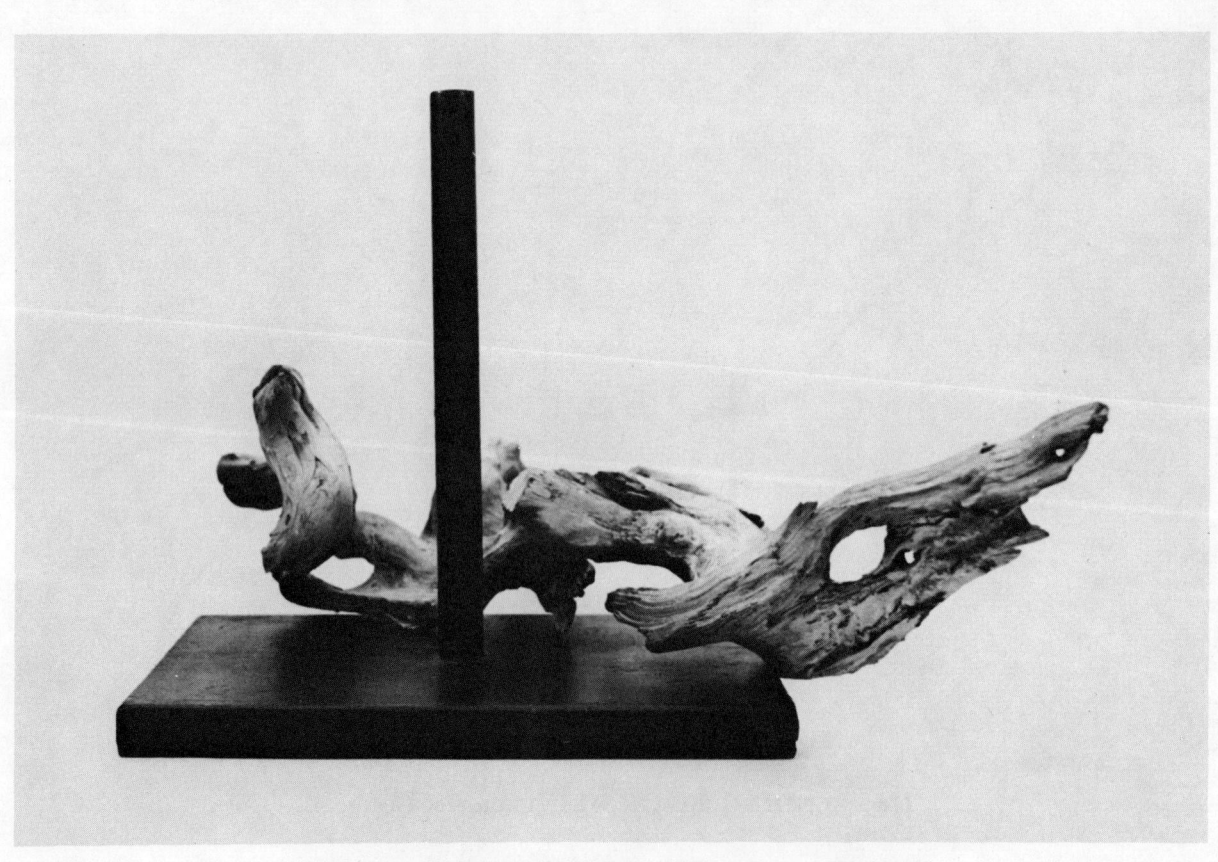

119 MOUNTING WOOD (Photo by Richard Hong)

Basic Mechanics

The use of one pinholder turned upside down on another to obtain additional bottom weight for an arrangement is also shown in plate 117.

Aqua picks are another useful piece of basic mechanics; they are small plastic vials with a rubber cap which has a hole in it for the flower stem. They may be anchored by means of clay or wire to driftwood and weathered wood to provide water for a short-stemmed flower. They may also be utilized on a wooden dowel or branch. Small plastic pill bottles can be substituted for aqua picks.

The interesting forms of the Scotch broom in plate 118 were anchored to a branch in the cup-pinholder by means of a gas or water hose clamp from the hardware store and a screw driver. This is a new technique with which I have been experimenting with very satisfactory results; it is a quick and easy way to balance a heavy branch. Just because a gadget was not designed for flower arrangers does not mean that it cannot be utilized by the creative arranger. (The clamps are available in a wide variety of sizes.)

Weathered wood may be mounted on a rod or dowel inserted into a base, as in plate 119. Although this is a strong, sturdy, stable technique, it is not a permanent mount and thus has the added advantage of coming apart for both storage and transportation.

Bandaid clear tape from the drug store is another material not designed for the arranger, but which has excellent possibilities for wiring leaves,

120 **WIRING A LEAF (Photo by Richard Hong)**

as in plate 120. Since it has wet strength and does not lift off in dampness, it can be used anywhere in a floral composition.

All in all, a knowledgeable horticulturist with an eye for line and design, a fertile mind, and a deft touch can have a ball with flower arranging. Lack of knowledge should not be a permanent problem. Once you are over the first hurdle of getting started, each additional jump becomes easier and should lead you further along the road to enjoyment and satisfaction in your own creative efforts.

9
Occasions for Flower Arranging

It would be difficult to find the occasion for which some type of flower arrangement would not be appropriate, for the intrinsic beauty and qualities of plant material can add much to our joy and soften our sorrows. Creative arrangements need know no season, and the world is full of exciting materials just waiting to be used.

Flowers at the door always present a welcome sight, whether in a May basket in the spring, or in a wreath or swag at holiday season. In plate 121, strawflowers were wired to a flat basket which was hung at the door. Pampas grass and velvety kalanchoe leaves from a house plant were also used for color, form, and a variety of textures.

Flowers at the table are an expected addition to most festive occasions. In plate 122, "Fall Buffet," cut ti leaves and three cat-tails in a cup-pinholder were used on an iron handmade "container." The blue ribbon table features Dansk plates, handmade amber Mexican glasses blown through a pierced iron collar, an iron casserole on a bronze hotplate, and a gold-colored Belgian tablecloth with black linen napkins.

The Halloween table centerpiece in plate 123 features orange tritoma (red hot pokers), Chinese lantern and Scotch broom with a sculptured teakwood black cat and three orange candles in a brass Indian candleholder on a black scroll base. A black lacquer cake plate, birch snack trays, black Bennington mugs, and orange linen napkins on a black linen tablecloth complete the composition, designed for a table-setting lecture.

121 **STRAWFLOWERS AND BASKET (Photo by James Swan)**

Occasions for Flower Arranging

122 FALL BUFFET (Photo by Bill Sevecke)

A table centerpiece, however, can also be simple and uncontrived in appearance, as is the arrangement in plate 124. The marigolds were arranged in a glass vase in a low horizontal composition, with all four sides presenting a similar facade. This type of arrangement, using one variety of flower and its own foliage, contains more plant material than would be required in a line or line-mass type of composition.

Gladioli, available at any season of the year, were used in plate 125. They also would be suitable for a table centerpiece, for some of the flowers and foliage face in each direction. The use of two matching ceramic containers in this Futakabu Shoka makes it possible to have as much interest in the back as in the front, while utilizing a minimum amount of material, in this case four spikes and their own leaves.

Arrangements can also suggest or commemorate an event as in "Bon Voyage" in plate 126. Eucalyptus and white phlox were massed to compensate for the textures and pattern of the Oriental rug and brick fireplace. In a "natural" setting, a busy background calls for heavier line and stronger treatment. A thin linear quality would wash out and make the arrangement difficult to see or enjoy.

In plate 127, the pewter angel provides a dominant motif suitable for a buffet or hall table Christmas arrangement. Three date palm spathes

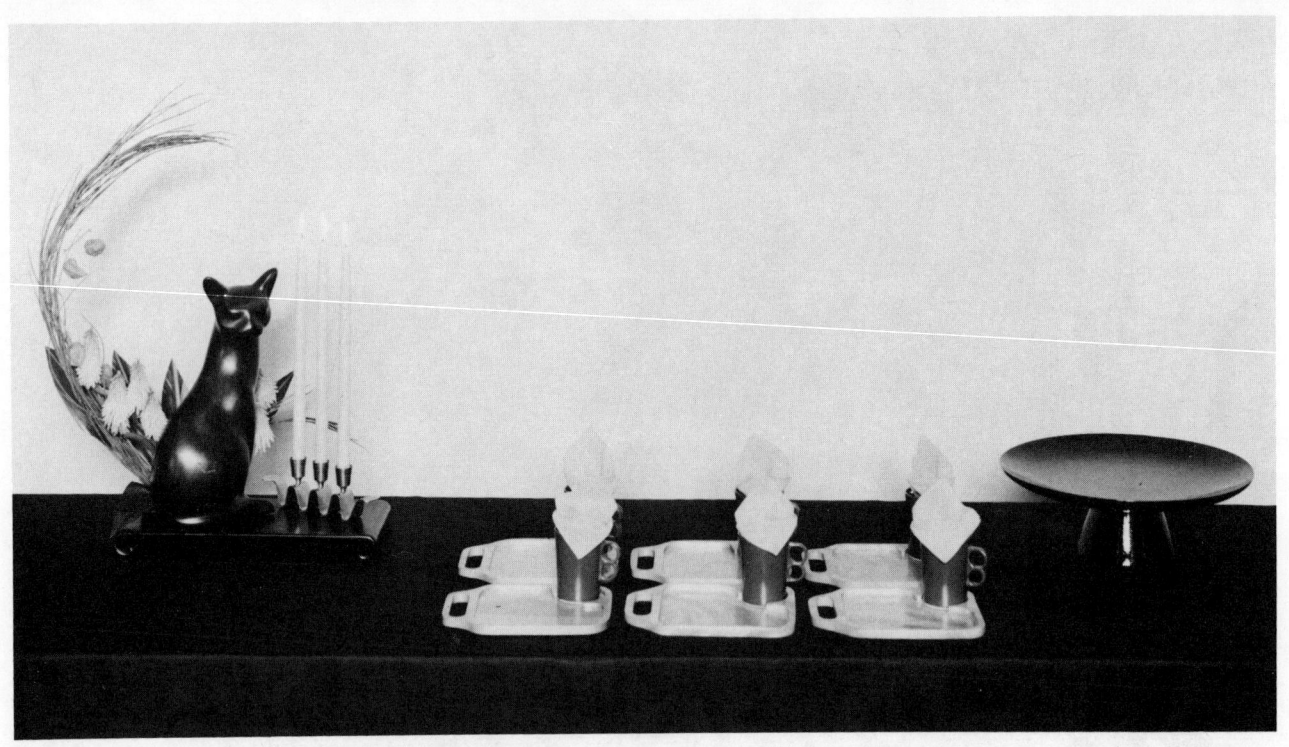

123 **HALLOWEEN TABLE** (Photo by Bill Sevecke)

124 **BOUQUET OF MARIGOLD** (Photo by James Swan)

125 FUTAKABU SHOKA WITH GLADIOLI
(Photo by James Swan)

sprayed silver and some small styrofoam balls threaded on a heavy wire add the linear interest. The "flowers" are small dried fungi rolled into a trumpet shape. All of the materials used in this long-lasting holiday composition were dried.

126 BON VOYAGE (Photo by Butler Studios)

Plate 128 was a blue ribbon arrangement interpreting one of the arts. The sculptured figure of a lute player by Rima, the space-enclosing bent strap metal and the freeform base, all painted green-bronze, were foils for the golden yellow gladioli. This composition would also be suitable for a strum-along party or an after-the-recital party, placed on a buffet table, sideboard, foyer table, or mantel.

Although plate 129, entitled "The Contemporary Spirit," was a blue ribbon arrangement from the New York Symposium at the Metropolitan Museum of Art, it still is suitable for almost any home. Bent strap metal was used again to enclose space in a geometric form and to repeat the rectangular quality of the brown container by Mimi Tripani, its rectangular area of dark-green glaze, and the rectangular black base. Holes were drilled in the vase to hold the metal properly.

Since the word "contemporary" does not mean "abstract" or "way out," the dried seed pods from the gingerbread palm were assembled into a rather traditional curved but sweeping line with green-bronze leucothoe and exciting speckled hybrid lilies as an accent. This arrangement, which does not have great radial depth, would be suitable for any shallow area which could carry a large composition.

The tall linear gladioli and bamboo used in plate 130 in the brown glazed circular Japanese container with a hole in it would not be suitable where radial depth is limited, for the very nature of a basic Shoka designates front-to-back thrust and movement. Thus, placement and subsequent enjoyment of any composition at home or in a show is greatly influenced by the type of design created.

"Ballet," plate 131, is another interpretive arrangement suitable for innumerable home situations and occasions. The container is a piece of bent metal tubing threaded with string after holes were drilled in it and into the base; it took many trial and error attempts to do this before I was satisfied with the bent forms and the string design created. Two strelitzia ballet dancers and a furled ti leaf were the fresh materials used in a cup-pinholder.

In my constructions, I always try to carry an idea from its inception and theme to its composition and completion so that there is a complete interplay of all of the parts and no part is completely alone, regardless of the materials used—fresh or organic, bio-morphic or man-made. I think that this is the true key to success in the use of the many and varied materials which are available to us.

In "Freedom," a blue ribbon arrangement from a New York State Judges' Council show (plate 132), there is a strong backward and diagonal pull of the welded chain, breaking away into a front-to-back depth relationship and swinging into the bent rod. The upward flight of the birds-of-paradise (strelitzia), reinforced by the vertical

127 PEWTER ANGEL (Photo by James Swan)

128 THE LUTE PLAYER (Photo by James Forney)

129 **THE CONTEMPORARY SPIRIT** (Photo by Colonel Louis Frohman)

which are attached to the ceiling above. Mobiles, of course, have mobility, but may be self-contained. Stabiles have come to mean those sculptures or arrangements which have arrested motion, but look poised for flight, as is plate 85.

The Pop Art hand in "Fruit Bowl" (plate 134) is another arrangement featuring fruit and vegetables. Some long-lasting galax leaves, fresh grapes, two apples, and the candles are the component parts of this whimsical composition.

When you have a good container or construction, it is often worth trying to use it in different ways. It is also perfectly legitimate to enter it in different shows, provided you do not repeat the same composition in it.

Compare plate 135, "Restraint," and plate 136, "Exuberance." The container is the same but the arrangements are totally different in concept and

130 GLADIOLI AND BAMBOO (Photo by James Swan)

use of yucca foliage, adds another note of contrast, tension and action.

At almost any time of the year, but particularly in the fall, a self-contained mobile, as in plate 133, can become an exciting decoration. Three magnolia leaves wired together with Christmas ornament hangers and two bronze football chrysanthemums are the main features. The fresh grapes, balanced on the top and the bottom, may be eaten by family and guests without disturbing the overall stability of this design.

Basically, the difference between "stabiles" and "mobiles" is comparable to that of stalagmites, which are attached to a cave floor, and stalactites,

131 BALLET (Photo by Alwood Harvey)

132 **FREEDOM** (Photo by George E. Ernst)

133 **MAGNOLIA MOBILE** (Photo by James Swan)

Occasions for Flower Arranging 155

handling, although both won blue ribbons in shows.

In "Restraint," the spike of prim white gladiolus is enfolded and confined by the space-restraining quality and line of the prickly cactus.

In "Exuberance," the heliconia exerts a strong vertical thrust and the placement of the monstera philodendron leaves adds dynamic tension, color, and spatial fluidity to the exuberant design.

Thus, there are many standards and criteria for creating and enjoying a flower arrangement—artistic criteria, horticultural perfection, aesthetics, interpretation, use, and even the purely subjective ones of preference. All are valid. But the more we know about all aspects of an art, the more enjoyment and understanding we will receive. Our points of view may differ, as so well expressed in a little poem by George H. Preston:

> If you look up and I look down
> Upon the biggest man in town,
> You'll see his head and ears and nose,
> I'll see his feet and knees and toes.
> And though it is one man we see,
> You'll swear he's "A," I'll swear he's "B."

Yet there is room for every sincere approach in the overall enjoyment available to all of us in truly seeing and creating beauty in the world around us.

134 **POP ART FRUIT BOWL** (Photo by James Swan)

135 **RESTRAINT** (Photo by Bill Sevecke)

136 **EXUBERANCE (Photo by Alwood Harvey)**

Index

ABALONE SHELLS, 28, 29
abstract geometric forms, 34, 35
abstractions, 53, 56
abundance, 41
acetic acid, 92
accessory, 17, 27
acorn caps, 96, 98
ACORN CAPS AND CONE FLOWERS, 96, 98
acorns, 53, 55
acrylic paint, 114, 117
aesthetics, 41
African daisies, 92
after-image, 27
AFTERMATH OF AN INDIAN RAID, 93, 94
AFTER THE BOAT RACE, 89
air drying, 93, 96, 102, 104
ALL FOLIAGE, 114, 117
allium, 62, 63, 120, 123
Allium gigantium, 122, 123
alocasia, 71
aloes, 71, 73
aluminum, 50
aluminum wire, 127
amaryllis, 89
ammonia, 114
ampelopsis, 77
andromeda, 58, 60
anemone, 102, 103
annealed (metals), 127
Anri, 20, 21
anthurium, 56, 69, 71, 96, 99
anti-freeze, 102
antler, 127
APOLLO—THE AGE OF AQUARIUS, 137, 138
apple, crab, 57, 59
APPLES, 34, 35
apples, 152, 155
apple blossom, 57
aqua pick, 35, 36, 43, 45, 50, 143
arbitrary rules, 53

Archimedes, 50
arrangement, line mass, 145, 148
arrangement, mass, 145, 146
arrangements, size, 126
arranging, 9, 143
art, 11, 50, 138, 148, 150, 155
artemisia, 93
artichoke, 105, 106, 112
artificial fruits and vegetables, 135, 136
artistic efforts, 50
artistic creed, 93
Ashcan school of art, 27
ASPIRATION, 101
aspirin, 92
assemblage, 31
AS YOU LIKE IT, 51, 53
automatic responses, 41
automobile body repair shop, 107, 127
A WALK IN THE WOODS, 114, 118
azalea, 22, 24, 102, 103

baby's breath, 93
background, your, 17, 32
bacterial development, 92
balance, 56
BALLET, 148, 152
bamboo, 58, 61, 62, 66, 67, 90, 112, 148, 152
BAMBOO AND FAN-TAIL WILLOW, 61, 62
bamboo, native, 107, 109
Barton, Mrs. Osa Mae, 37
base, 20, 21, 23, 30, 31, 46, 56, 57, 58, 71, 74, 77, 84, 98, 101, 142, 143, 152, 156
base, bamboo, 52
base, burl, 58, 60, 96, 100, 108, 109, 112, 114, 118, 134, 135
base, cryptomeria, 65, 130, 131
base, freeform, 24, 29, 69, 122, 123, 148, 149, 150
base, marble, 90, 92
base, oval, 36

base, rectangular, 28, 67, 68, 75, 91, 99, 111, 125, 127, 133, 148, 151, 153, 154, 157
base, round, 47, 54, 76, 85, 124, 155
base, scroll, 88, 144, 146
base, shingle, 102, 104, 135, 136
base, wooden, 93, 95, 103, 105, 106, 114, 117, 130, 131
basket, 138, 144
BASKET AND CERAMIC CONTAINERS, 138
bean, castor, 57
beauty, 11, 27, 31, 41, 43, 57, 83, 138, 144, 155
begonia, angelwing, 69, 71
begonia, Joe Hayden, 53, 54, 69, 71
begonia, rex, 46, 57, 71, 114, 117
being able, 50
Beloperone guttata, 66, 69, 87, 89
BENDING BRANCHES, 141
berries, 93
Berry, Daniel, 23
binoculars, 56
BIRD AND BAMBOO, 109
BIRD AND PACHYSANDRA, 108
BIRD MOBILE, 35, 36
birds-of-paradise, 148, 153
Blake, William, 9
BLAST OFF, 88, 89
blue ribbon, 20, 21, 23, 30, 31, 46, 47, 48, 49, 51, 53, 57, 58, 59, 66, 67, 69, 71, 73, 76, 77, 83, 84, 88, 89, 91, 92, 93, 95, 101, 102, 103, 112, 114, 117, 118, 127, 130, 131, 145, 148, 149, 150, 151, 152, 153, 156, 157
BON VOYAGE, 145, 148
borax, 96
botanist, 56
BOUILLABAISSE, 130, 131
bouquet, 41, 42, 86, 145, 146
BOUQUET OF MARIGOLD, 145, 146
boxer, 71, 73
branch, balance, 142, 143
branches, 17, 18, 26, 35, 36, 43, 47, 52, 57, 58, 59, 60, 61, 62, 70, 72, 79, 81, 86, 98, 101, 102, 103, 107, 108, 112, 114, 118, 139, 141, 142, 143
branches, budded, 78, 107, 108
branches, dormant, 57, 58
branches, dried, 26, 27, 36, 46, 47, 101, 112, 118
branches, forked, 140
branches, inverted, 114, 116
brass tubing, 127
Brassica oleracea, 62
bricks, 20, 21
bromeliads, 66
BROOM AND CROCUS, 127, 129
Bruegel, Pieter, 32
Brussels sprouts, 63, 65
Bryce Canyon, 22
buds, 43, 57, 71
buffet arrangements, 145, 148, 149, 150
Butler Studios, 148

cabbage, 62
cactus, 66, 68, 69, 71, 155, 156
cake plate, 144, 146
caladium, 71
calatheas, 134, 135

Calder, Alexander, 22, 35
camera, 56, 138
camouflage, 22, 27
candles, 55, 105, 144, 146, 152, 155
cans, 135, 139
CANTALOUPE AND CORN CONTAINERS, 135
cantilevered weight, 140, 141
capillary action, 86, 105, 139, 140
CAPRICORN, 113, 114
carborundum bit, 126
carnations, 90, 92
carrots, 63, 66
casserole, 144, 145
cat-tails, 46, 53, 71, 72, 74, 93, 96, 137, 138, 141, 144, 145
cedrus glauca atlantica, 127
Cellini, 50
center of interest, 127
centerpiece, 145, 146, 147
cereus, night-blooming, 66, 69, 71, 73, 84, 85
Cezanne, Paul, 33, 35
Chabana, 41
chain, welded, 148, 153
changes, 35
charcoal, in water, 78
chemist, 56
cherry blossom, 57
chestnut, horse, 52, 53, 114, 118
CHIANTI BOTTLE CONTAINER, 138
china, 46
CHINESE LANTERN, 93, 95
Chinese lantern, 93, 95, 144, 146
chlorinated household bleach, 105
chrysanthemum, 36, 53, 54, 57, 59, 86, 96, 101, 125, 127, 152, 154
CHRYSANTHEMUM AND OAK, 86
CIRCLES, 120, 124
clay, 135, 139, 140, 143
clay, self-hardening, 131
cleanliness, 92
clorox, 105
clover, 27, 28
coat hanger wire, 35
COCONUT HULL CONTAINERS, 126, 127
Colonial flower arrangers, 50
color, 27, 41, 46, 53, 86, 102, 114, 117
color, analogous, 63, 66
colors, fall, 63
color unity, 63, 66
commonplace, 53
compatibility, 46, 126
composition, horizontal, 145, 146
concepts, 152, 156, 157
Concrete Poetry, 17, 19
conditioning, 21, 46, 83–92
conservation list, 21
constructions, 120, 148
consumers of art, 22
container and composition, 46
container, broken, 138
containers, 27, 34, 35, 46, 47, 48, 56, 57, 58, 59, 61, 62, 120–139, 152, 156
CONTAINERS, CLASSICAL BRONZE, 121
CONTAINERS, CONTEMPORARY CERAMIC, 121
containers, glass, 134, 135

Index

containers, Japanese, 57, 58, 71, 72, 148, 152
containers, multimouthed, 48, 127
containers, size, 126
containers, wood, 86, 131, 132
contemporary arranging, 120
CONTEMPORARY SPIRIT, 148, 151
contrast of opposites, 28
Cook, Howard C., 105
copper, 50
copper sulphate, 114
copper tubing, 35, 36, 120, 127, 128
COPPER TUBING CONTAINER, 127, 128
copying, 50
corn meal, 96
corn shucks and tassels, 57
cotton flowers, 102
craftsmanship, 31
crassulacaea, 71
creativity, 21, 37, 43, 50, 53, 56, 138, 144
crescent design, 51, 53
criteria for evaluation, 17, 21, 28–37, 155
crocus, 58, 61, 62, 127, 129
cropping, 31
crowding, 41
Cryptocereus anthonyanus, 66, 68, 69, 71
cucumbers, 63, 66
cutting under water, 84, 85
Cyperaceae, 66, 67
CZECHOSLOVAKIA, 125, 127

daffodils, 34, 35, 89
dahlias, 83, 84, 120, 124
DAHLIAS, CERAMIC, AND METAL, 84
daisies, 17, 18, 27
Dali, Salvador, 31
Dansk plates, 89, 144, 145
DATE PALM AND GIRL, 107, 110
Da Vinci, Leonardo, 32
day lily, 71, 74, 83, 84, 85
defoliation, 92
de Kooning, Willem, 31
depth, 148, 153
depth, radial, 58, 61, 62, 148, 151, 152
design, 28, 41, 46, 56, 86, 92, 148
design, elements, 32
design, modern, 20, 24, 26, 28, 29, 45, 47, 48, 50, 58, 67, 68, 74, 75, 76, 84, 85, 87, 88, 90, 91, 94, 99, 101, 104, 106, 108, 109, 110, 111, 112, 113, 115, 117, 118, 119, 120, 122, 123, 124, 125, 133, 134, 137, 149, 150, 151, 152, 153, 154, 155, 156, 157
design, preconceived, 43, 53
design, principles, 32
details, attention to, 50
Devil's claw, 66
dieffenbachia, 66
discoloration (in drying), 96
distinction, 53
DIVIDED SHOKA, 43, 44
dock, 21, 75
dominance and contrast, 32
dominances, multiple, 125, 127
dominant area, 53
dominant motif, 145, 149
dormancy, prolonging, 78, 81, 82

DRIED FLOWERS, 96, 97
driftwood, 27, 28, 66, 68, 78, 80, 93, 94, 107–119, 139
drilling holes, 126
Drouais, Jean Germain, 33, 35
drug store, 143
drying, 93–101
drying time, 96, 101
dry material, 53, 54, 96, 100
Dürer, Albrecht, 31, 32
Dutch masters, 32
dynamic tension, 46, 47, 50, 155, 157

Earthworks, 22
echeveria, 43, 71, 114, 115
eclectic taste, 53
ECOLOGY, 131, 133
EGYPTIAN TREE ONIONS, 62, 63
electric drill, 126, 148, 151
elements and principles, 43, 50
elements, essential, 56
Elmer's glue, 114
embellishments, 46
enjoyment, 17
equipment, 139–143
Ernst, George E., 24, 26, 29, 50, 52, 58, 69, 79, 80, 81, 84, 99, 100, 102, 110, 111, 115, 116, 124, 133, 135, 137, 140, 141, 153
eucalyptus, 22, 24, 101, 131, 132, 145, 148
EUCALYPTUS RIKKA, 131, 132
Euphorbia pedilanthus, 66
euphorbias, 83
evaluation, self, 56
evergreens, 17, 18, 58, 60
evergreens, preservative, 105
everlastings, 93
exotic material, 53
exotic tropicals, 50
experiences, 28
EXPERIMENT IN BROWN, 102, 104
exposure, 37
EXUBERANCE, 155, 157
eye, perceptive, 57

fabrics, 46, 56
FALL, 57, 59
FALL BOUNTY, 63, 65
FALL BUFFET, 144, 145
FASCIATED MULLEIN AND WOOD, 75
FIELD AND ROADSIDE FLOWERS, 21, 23
field and roadside material, 21, 23
Fields, Melinda, 26, 27, 30, 31, 53, 55, 66, 69, 96, 98
Fields, Nanette, 51, 52, 53, 58, 60, 78, 79, 80, 96, 97
figurine, 20, 21, 30, 31, 35, 36, 54, 56, 58, 60, 73, 78, 80, 87, 89, 96, 98, 101, 107, 108, 109, 110, 112, 130, 131, 144, 145, 146, 149
fireplace, 145, 148
FISH MOBILE, 27, 28
floats, 130, 131
floundering, 50
flower arranger, 50
flower arrangements, 56, 144
Flower Dri, 96
flowers at the door, 144
flowers, holding over, 82

flowers, roadside, 92
flowers, short stemmed, 86
flower show, 28
Floralife, 92
FLYING TRAPEZE, 50
foliage, 43, 53, 54
foliage, excess, 92
foliage, horsechestnut, 125, 127
foliage, pattern, 69, 71
forcing bloom, 78, 79, 80
form, 53
form, geometric, 148, 151
formulas for drying, 96
Forney, James, 150
forsythia, 35, 36, 71, 72, 78, 88, 89
foundation plantings, 58, 60
FREEDOM, 148, 153
free-form design, 43
freesia, 57, 58
free-style design, 43
fresh and dried material, 17
fresh plant material, 51, 53
frogs, 41
Frohman, Colonel Louis, 151
Froman, Robert, 17, 19
fruit, 27, 152, 155
fruit, foliage, flowers, 35
fruits and vegetables, cut, 135
fumes, 137, 138
fungus, 112, 114, 118, 148, 149
FUTAKABU SHOKA WITH GLADIOLI, 145, 147

galax, 57, 152, 155
Galileo, 50
Garvey, C. Everett, 20
GENDAI RIKKA, 22, 24
generation gap, 31
geranium, 20, 21, 43, 45, 131, 133
Gibbiflora metallica, 114, 115
Gilson, Ginnie, 66, 69, 78, 79, 130, 131
ginger, torch, 114, 119
GIRL ASLEEP, 33, 35
GIRL HOLDING A FLOWER BASKET, 33, 35
gladioli, 26, 27, 28, 29, 52, 53, 66, 67, 76, 77, 111, 112, 127, 130, 131, 145, 147, 148, 150, 152, 155, 156
GLADIOLI AND BAMBOO, 148, 152
glass, 46, 138
glass floats, 27, 28
glass, plate, 131
glass, slag, 131
glass, tubes, 131
globe amaranth, 93
glycerine, 101, 102, 103, 104
glycerinized eucalyptus, 131, 132
glycerinizing time, 102
God's bounty, 11
golden rod, 93
gourds, 62
GOURMET, THE, 21, 22
Goya, Francisco José de, 93
grapes, 113, 114, 152, 154, 155
"grapes," 53, 55, 63, 65
grape vines, 77

grasses, 25, 27, 93, 96, 97
Greek and Roman sculptures, 31
Greek sculptors, 92
green, 53
Green Gard Micronized Iron, 105
GREENWICH VILLAGE, 20

Haeger container, 62, 63
HALLOWEEN, 53, 55
HALLOWEEN TABLE, 144, 146
Halper, Estelle, 58, 61, 62, 71, 74, 76, 77, 84, 85, 102, 104
hardware store, 143
Harvey, Alwood, 18, 27, 30, 34, 43, 44, 46, 47, 49, 51, 55, 60, 66, 69, 88, 91, 94, 97, 108, 109, 122, 123, 127, 152, 157
heather, 22, 24, 30, 31
HELICONIA, 120, 122
heliconia, 120, 122, 155, 157
hemerocallis, 71, 74, 83, 84, 85
hen-and-chickens, 71, 107, 109
hibiscus, 93
high school gardeners, juniors, 26, 27, 30, 51, 52, 53, 55, 60, 69, 80, 97, 98
hobby shops, 131, 133
holes drilled, 126, 148, 151
HOLOCAUST, 96, 99
honesty, 93
Hong, Richard, 15, 42, 121, 126, 128, 131, 133, 135, 138, 142, 143
HOSE CLAMP, 142, 143
hosta, 70, 71, 102, 104
HOSTA, PHLOX, AND LARCH, 70, 71
houseplant foliage, 20, 43, 45, 48, 53, 54, 67, 68, 69, 73, 74, 85, 87, 113, 115, 117, 133, 136, 144
house plants, 46, 53, 54, 57, 69, 71–73, 114, 117, 144
hydrangea, 46, 71, 72, 91, 92, 102, 104

idea, development, 56
ideal woman, 31
Ikebana, 92
IKENOBO RIKKA, 17, 18
Ikenobo school, 141, 142
Ikenobo, Senei, 120
impact, 50
Impossible Art, 22
Impressionists, 27
INDIAN WAR DANCE, 112
inspiration, 56
International Flower Show, 26, 27, 52, 53
international party, 120, 123, 125, 127
IN THE ORIENTAL MANNER, 46, 49
iris, 17, 18, 22, 24, 83, 92
iris, bearded, 81, 82
iris foliage, 102, 104
iris, Siberian, 75
ishuike, 92
ivy, grape, 113, 114

Japanese design, 17, 18, 22
jeweler's rouge, 131, 133
Josephine, Empress, 35
judges, 21
judging, 11
juniors, high school gardeners, 26, 27, 30, 51, 52, 53, 55, 60, 69, 80, 97, 98

Index

juniper, 58, 60, 105

kalanchoes, 71, 144
kale, flowering, 62
Karo syrup, 105
Kemble, Connie, 46, 48
KNOCK-OUT PUNCH, 71, 73
knowledge, 28, 37, 46, 50, 53
kubari, 140, 141

landscape, 32, 35
landscape painting, 32
larch, 70, 71
laterals, 83, 84
LAVA AND OSMUNDA CONTAINERS, 131, 133
lava rock, 131, 133
lavender, 93
learning, 50, 53
leaves, 139
leaves, wiring, 143
leucothoe, 46, 148, 151
liatris, 93
light, 46
LIGHTNING, 46, 47
lilac, 78, 79, 93, 141
lilies, 9, 66, 68
lilies, calla, 27, 50, 66, 69, 89
lilies, rubrum, 56
lilies, speckled, 148, 151
lilies, umbellatum, 46, 49
lily, foliage, 46, 49
limitations, 50
line, 43, 46, 47, 57, 86, 148, 152, 153
line, crescent, 51, 60
line, heavy, 145, 148
line mass, 23, 43, 58, 63, 65, 78, 80, 100, 105, 114, 115, 116, 130, 148
line material, 75, 76, 77, 78, 79, 80, 81, 82, 134, 135
linens, 89, 92, 144, 145, 146
line, radiating, 71, 74
line, reversing, 53
line, space restraining, 155, 156
line, strong, 131, 133
line, thin, 145, 148
line, traditional, 148, 151
LINES, 46
lines, crossing, 53
lines, parallel, 53
lines, swirling, 107, 110
linseed oil, 114
l. p. record, 26, 27
lumber yards, 131, 133
lunaria, 93
LUTE PLAYER, 148, 150

Macbeth, 27
magnolia, 46, 102, 103, 105
MAGNOLIA, ANEMONE, AND AZALEA, 102, 103
magnolia leaves, 152, 154
MAGNOLIA MOBILE, 152, 154
main line, 46, 49
maple, 57, 58, 105
maple whip, 101

marantha, 66
marigold, 145, 146
martynia, 27, 28, 62, 130, 131
mass arrangements, 42, 43, 97, 116, 146
masterpieces, 53
materials, choice of, 93
materials, distinctive, 57
materials, dry, 56, 134, 135, 141, 148, 149
materials, objective, 50
materials, subjective, 50
mechanics, 46, 53, 56, 139–143
metal, 27, 28, 29, 34, 35, 36, 43, 45, 46, 50, 67, 84, 88, 89, 90, 91, 92, 96, 99, 120, 122, 123, 125, 127, 128, 144, 145, 148, 152, 153, 156, 157
metal screening, 127, 128, 129
metal tubing, 148, 152
Metropolitan Museum of Art, 32, 33, 148, 151
Mexican glass, 144, 145
Michelangelo, 21
Middle Ages, 21
MILKWEED PODS, 96, 100
milky sap, 83
mind, open, 56
MINIATURE, 30, 31
miniature, 30, 31, 127
MIRROR, THE, 21, 22
mirror, 56
mistakes, 53
mobiles, 27, 28, 35, 36, 63, 66, 152, 154
modern artists, 21
modern design, 20, 28, 29, 34, 45, 47, 48, 50, 67, 68, 69, 73, 74, 75, 76, 84, 85, 88, 90, 91, 94, 96, 99, 101, 104, 106, 108, 109, 110, 111, 112, 113, 114, 117, 122, 123, 124, 125, 126, 133, 134, 137, 149, 150, 151, 152, 153, 155, 156, 157
MODERN MUSIC, 66, 67
Mondrian, Piet, 35
monstera, 71
Moore, Henry, 35
Moribana, 22, 49, 63, 95, 120
Moses, 21
moth, 22
mounting, 127, 142, 143
Mount Rushmore, 22
mugs, Bennington, 144, 146
mullein, 20, 21, 23, 46, 75
music, 17
MUSICAL VIOLINIST, 54

Nageire, 78, 79, 86, 119, 140, 141
NAGEIRE OF LILAC AND PINE, 78, 79
National Council of State Garden Clubs, 21, 37
native plant material, 21
nature (variety in), 57
nature's discards, 127
nature's principles, 27
nature's sculptures, 27
nature's treasures, 107, 108, 109, 112, 113–119, 127
nature's tricks, 22
nepenthes, 71, 74
new forms, 31
new ideas, 37
new materials, 46, 50
New York City, 21

N.Y.S. Annual meeting, 92
N.Y.S. Judges Council, 96, 120, 122, 148, 153
N.Y. Symposium, 148, 151
NIGHT BLOOMING CEREUS, 66, 69
NISHUIKE OF SPIREA AND IRIS, 78, 81
NISHUIKE SCREEN CONTAINER, 127, 128
nudes, 31

oak, 105
oak branch, 96, 98
oak foliage, 86
oasis, 41, 138, 139, 140
objets trouvés, 27, 28, 29
occasions, 141–158
OKRA, 62, 64
okra, 58, 61, 62, 64
onions, 57
onions, Egyptian tree, 62, 63, 135, 136
Op Art, 22
OPEN HOUSE, 135, 136
open mind, 37
Oriental rug, 145, 148
osmunda fiber, 131, 133
oven, home, 131

pachysandra, 107, 108
paint, spray, 139, 140
painters, 22, 27, 31, 32, 33, 35, 50
painting, 31
palm, 120, 124
palm, cocoanut, 96, 99
palm, date, 102, 107, 110
palm, date spathes, 145, 149
palmetto, clipped, 93, 94, 131, 132
palm, fish-tail, 69, 71
palm, gingerbread, 46, 49, 148, 151
pampas grass, 20, 21, 43, 45, 71, 93, 94, 144
pampas grass stems, 91, 92, 96
pandanus, 66, 89
papyrus, 66, 67
PARTY FOR SWINGERS, 26, 27
parsley, 46
pattern, 53
PENTHOUSE GLAMOUR, 90, 92
PEONIES AND WOOD, 84
peony, 56, 83, 84
peppers, 63, 66
perishable medium, 46
personal experience, 50
perspective of time, 31, 56
pet shop, 131
petunia, 27
pewter, 127
PEWTER ANGEL, 145, 148, 149
PFITZER JUNIPER, CANDLE, AND WOOD, 105
philodendron, 43, 71
philodendron, monstera, 155, 157
philodendron, Swiss cheese, 69, 71, 135, 136
phlox, 70, 71, 145, 148
photographer, 56
physical imbalance, 35
PI IN THE SKY, 91, 92
piano, 46, 49

Picasso, Pablo, 21, 22
pine, 51, 53, 78, 79, 141
pineapples, 62, 65
pinecone, 105
pinecone flowers, 96, 98
PING-PONG, ANYONE?, 76, 77
ping-pong balls, 77
pinholder, bottom weight, 142, 143
pinholder, diffusing it, 139
pinholder, extension, 141, 142
PINHOLDERS, 141, 142
pinholders, 41, 131, 132, 135, 136, 139, 140, 141
pinholders, care of, 92
pinholders, cup, 20, 21, 26, 27, 53, 54, 57, 58, 59, 60, 66, 67, 69,
   75, 88, 89, 90, 92, 93, 98, 105, 106, 107, 108, 110, 111, 112, 113,
   114, 116, 117, 120, 122, 123, 124, 127, 129, 130, 131, 137, 138,
   139, 140, 141, 142, 143, 144, 145, 148, 152
plant material, 56, 139, 140
plant material (manipulation), 141
plant material, picking, 83
plant material, preserving, 46, 93–106, 139
plants, field and roadside, 75, 76, 77
plants, perennial, 70, 71, 72, 73, 74, 75
plastic filaments, 131
plastic pill bottles, 143
plastic rods, 105, 106, 131, 133
plastic sheets, 131
plastic tubing, 105, 106, 131
plastics, 46, 50
platinum, 50
plumber's lead, 127
Pocantico Hills Estate, 120, 123, 125, 127
podocarpus, 102
PODOCARPUS AND COTTON FLOWERS, 102
pods, dried, 58, 61, 62, 64, 71, 75, 131, 132
pods, milkweed, 93, 96, 100
pods, Royal poinciana, 84, 85, 125, 127
poinsettias, 83
POP ART FRUIT BOWL, 152, 155
poppies, 75, 83
portrait, 31, 33, 35
pothos, 57
pot plant flowers, 86
POT PLANT FOLIAGE, 69, 71
pot plants, 66, 67, 68, 69, 71, 74
pottery, 46
Prado Museum, 31
preservative for evergreens, 105
Preston, George H., 155
profile, 53
PROFILE OF PLATE, 62
progress, 31
protea, 43, 44
pruning, 52, 53
psychedelic colors, 27
pumpkin container, 55
PUSSY WILLOW AND LILAC, 78, 80

Queen Anne's lace, 21, 23, 25, 27, 46, 70, 71, 93

raison d'être, 31, 46
RECORD, 27
Redouté, Pierre, 35

Index

RED SAILS IN THE SUNSET, 52, 53
RESTRAINT, 152, 156
reviving flowers, 92
RHUBARB, 57, 58
rhythm and balance, 31
Rikka, 17, 18, 22, 24, 25, 27, 58, 61, 62, 70, 71, 72, 103, 132
Rima, 107, 110, 148, 150
roadside material, 96, 100
roots, 53, 55, 71, 96, 99, 107, 134, 135
rope, 135
rose hips, 75, 93
rose petals, 46
roses, 9, 27, 51, 53
Ruddley, John, 9

salad bowl, 51, 53
salt, 96
sand, 96, 134, 135, 140
sandblasting, 107
sansevieria, 43, 46, 62, 65, 71, 73, 113, 114, 117
santolina, 93
saw, 135
saxifrage, 71, 72
SAXIFRAGE AND HYDRANGEA, 72
scale and proportion, 22, 31, 32, 46, 71
Schillaci, Edward, 112
scissors, 139, 140
Scotch broom, 127, 129, 131, 132, 142, 143, 144, 146
SEA, THE, 66, 68
sea fan, 66, 68
seasons, 50, 57
secondary line, 46, 49
seed pods, 43, 46, 49, 57, 62, 64, 93, 148, 151
selectivity, 41
self expression, 31, 41
SELF PORTRAIT, 31
September Morn, 31
Seurat, Georges, 31
Sevecke, Bill, 65, 67, 73, 89, 90, 101, 117, 118, 125, 145, 146, 156
shears, pruning, 139, 140
shellac, 105
shell, walnut, 127
shibui, 27
shin, 46, 49
SHIP AHOY, 111, 112
shock techniques, 50
Shoka (Ikenobo), 22, 44, 57, 58, 59, 64, 81, 102, 129, 136, 147, 148, 152
Shoka (Ikenobo Futakabu), 43, 44, 120, 145, 147
Shoka (Ikenobo Sanshuike), 102
show schedule, 17, 21
shrimp plant, 66, 69, 87, 89
SHRIMP PLANT AND FLUTE PLAYER, 87, 89
SHRIMP PLANT AND WOOD, 66, 69
shrubs, 46
silica gel, 96, 102
simplicity, 46, 50
skeletonizing leaves, 105, 106
skill, 56, 138
skunk cabbage, 114, 118
slate, 30, 31
Sloan, John, 27
soe, 46, 49

solids, 46
SOUP DE JOUR, 63, 66
SPACE AND FORM, 48
SPACE AND PATTERN, 35
spatial fluidity, 155, 157
spatial relationships, 35, 46, 48, 49, 53
spatial voids, 88, 89
spiraea, 78, 81, 82
sponge, 102, 104
spray, 92
SPRING, 57, 58
squash, 62, 65
stabiles, 112, 152
stability, physical, 140
stalks, 71
standards, 50
statice, 93
stems, long, 86
STILL LIFE, 33, 35
storage, dried material, 101
strap metal, 120, 124, 148, 150, 151
strawflowers, 93, 97, 144
STRAWFLOWERS AND BASKET, 144
STREET POEMS, 17, 19
strelitzia, 148, 152, 153
string, 148, 152
structurally sound, 31
STUDY IN TEXTURES, 84, 85
styrofoam, 135, 137, 138
styrofoam balls, 148, 149
succulents, 71, 114, 117
suiban, 120
sumac, 21, 75, 93
surface decorations, 131
Swan, James, 25, 28, 36, 45, 48, 54, 58, 59, 61, 62, 63, 64, 68, 69, 70, 72, 74, 75, 76, 85, 86, 87, 95, 98, 103, 104, 105, 106, 112, 112, 119, 129, 130, 132, 134, 136, 144, 146, 147, 149, 152, 154, 155
SWING YOUR PARTNER, 71, 74
Swiss cheese effect, 137, 138

table settings, 89, 144, 145, 146
tai, 46, 49
Takahashi, Mary, 17, 18
tansy, 93
tape, 139, 140
tape, Bandaid clear, 143
tapestries, 21
taxus, 71, 72
technique, 31
tertiary line, 46, 49
texture, 46, 53, 71, 86, 131, 134, 135
textures and pattern, 145, 148
TEXTURES AND TONES, 105, 106
thistles, 93
ti leaves, 43, 44, 57, 66, 67, 69, 71, 88, 89, 90, 92, 102, 103, 144, 145, 148, 152
TICK TACK TOE, 43, 45
TIN CAN CONTAINERS, 135
TIVOLI, 120, 123
tools, 50
TOOLS OF THE TRADE, 140
tooth picks, 63, 65, 135

TORCH GINGER AND WOOD, 46, 47, 114, 119
transitional material, 43
transpiration, 92
trays, snack, 144, 146
tree-cankers, 96, 100
trees, 57
trees, Birnam Woods, 27
Tripani, Mimi, 148, 151
tritoma, 88, 89, 144, 146
tomatoes, 63, 66
tulips, 42, 75, 89, 114, 116
TULIPS, 41, 42
TULIPS IN A VASE, 33, 35

understanding (a performer's), 17
Unicorn tapestries, 21
unity (of form and color), 63, 66
usubata, 46, 49, 120

VACATION MEMORIES, 127
Van Gogh, Vincent, 31
Van Ruisdael, Jacob, 32
variety, 46, 53
varnish, 114
vase, glass, 145, 146
vegetable, 46
vegetable garden, 58, 62, 63, 64, 65, 66
Venus de Milo, 31
Vermeer, Johannes, 33, 35
VERNAL EQUINOX, 112
vinegar, 92
vines, 43, 76, 77, 114, 118
vines, bent and knotted, 77
vine, wisteria, 57
violet foliage, 25, 27
Virginia creeper, 57, 76, 77, 130, 131
voids, 46

WALK IN THE WOODS, 114, 118
walnuts, 53
water, 92, 139, 140, 141, 143
water intake, 78

wax, 140
wax, liquid, 114
weathered wood, 21, 23, 46, 48, 62, 65, 66, 69, 75, 83, 84, 87, 89, 96, 100, 105, 107, 114, 116, 117, 118
weed killer, 75
WEED RIKKA, 25, 27
weeds, 25, 27, 46, 75, 93, 97
welding, 127
Westchester Art Workshop, 9, 107, 108
WHEATFIELDS, 32
willow, 43, 44, 46, 47
willow, basket-weaving, 71, 74
willow, cane-weaving, 84
willow, corkscrew, 58
willow, fan-tail, 58, 61, 62
willow, pussy, 22, 24, 78, 80
wilted flowers, 92
wilting, 83
WINTER, 58, 60
wire, 139, 140, 143, 148, 149
WIRING A LEAF, 143
wisteria, 28, 29, 77, 93
wood, 57, 58, 131, 133, 142, 143
WOOD AND ECHEVERIA, 114, 115
WOOD AND TULIPS, 114, 116
wood, bleached, 114
wood, blue, 114, 116
wood, cleaning, 107
WOOD CONTAINERS, 131
wood, mounting, 107, 111
wood, painted, 93, 95, 114
wood, stains, 114
wood, whittled, 114

yarrow, 93, 134, 135
YARROW AND CALATHEAS, 134, 135
yucca, 50, 91, 92, 96, 99, 101, 120, 122, 152, 153

zebra, 22
zebra plant, 69, 71
zinnias, 83, 92
zucchini, 46, 57, 63